Islamicate Cosmopolitan Spirit

Islamicate Cosmopolitan Spirit

Bruce B. Lawrence
Duke University
Durham, USA

WILEY Blackwell

Registered Office
John Wiley & Sons, Inc., 111 River Street, Hoboken, NJ 07030, USA

Editorial Office
111 River Street, Hoboken, NJ 07030, USA

For details of our global editorial offices, customer services, and more information about Wiley products visit us at www.wiley.com.

Wiley also publishes its books in a variety of electronic formats and by print-on-demand. Some content that appears in standard print versions of this book may not be available in other formats.

Library of Congress Cataloging-in-Publication Data
Names: Lawrence, Bruce B., author.
Title: Islamicate cosmopolitan spirit / Bruce B. Lawrence.
Description: Hoboken, NJ : John Wiley & Sons, 2021. | Series:
   Wiley-Blackwell manifestos | Includes bibliographical references and
   index. | Contents: Overview : a manifesto in 3 words and 6 chapters --
   Islamicate cosmopolitan spirit across time and space -- Eastward into
   India -- Westward into Spain -- Premodern Afro-Eurasia -- Persianate
   culture across the Indian ocean -- Islamicate cosmopolitan spirit beyond
   2020 -- Conclusion.
Identifiers: LCCN 2020058488 (print) | LCCN 2020058489 (ebook) | ISBN
   9781405155144 (paperback) | ISBN 9781118779996 (pdf) | ISBN
   9781118780008 (epub)
Subjects: LCSH: Islamic civilization. | Cosmopolitanism.
Classification: LCC DS36.88 .L395 2021 (print) | LCC DS36.88 (ebook) |
   DDC 909/.09767--dc23
LC record available at https://lccn.loc.gov/2020058488
LC ebook record available at https://lccn.loc.gov/2020058489

Cover image: © Alberto Manuel Urosa Toledano/Getty Images
Cover design by Wiley

Set in 11.5/14 Bembo Std by Integra Software Services, Pondicherry, India
Printed and bound by CPI Group (UK) Ltd, Croydon, CR0 4YY

C043289_070921

To Alber Husin
Gun-less Warrior for Peace
Exemplar Cosmopolitan for the Ages

Contents

Acknowledgments

The roll call of colleagues who helped shape this manifesto extends back several decades and crosses generations as well as continents. I would be remiss not to begin with the 1980 conference on Islamic studies organized by my late friend, Richard C. Martin of Arizona State University. Rich brought together older colleagues, such as James Kritzeck (my first teacher on Islam), Jacques Waardenburg, and Muhammad Abd ar-Rauf, along with younger scholars like William Graham, Marilyn Waldman, and Fred Denny, to rethink the field of Islamic studies beyond *Orientalism*. Said's book had just been published 2 years earlier (1978) and one of the several scholars invoked to chart a way beyond Orientalism was Marshall Hodgson. Fast forward 25 years and Rich Martin, along with Carl W. Ernst, organized a conference on Islam in Theory and Practice that centered on my work, and it highlighted Hodgson as the harbinger of a Muslim/Islamic/Islamicate cosmopolitan alternative to Orientalism. All the participants of that 2006 conference, later contributors to a book titled *Rethinking Islamic Studies: From Orientalism to Cosmopolitanism* (Columbia: University of South Carolina Press, 2010), deserve recognition and thanks: Ernst and Martin at the head of the list, followed by Vincent J. Cornell, Katherine P. Ewing, A. Kevin Reinhart, Omid Safi, Jamillah Karim, Charles Kurzman, Ijlal Naqvi, David Gilmartin, Abbas Barzegar, Louis A. Ruprecht, Jr., Tony K. Stewart, Scott Kugle, and Ebrahim Moosa. In 2008 I was awarded a Carnegie Scholars of Islam grant, allowing me to travel not just to Egypt and Ethiopia but also to Indonesia and the Philippines. My experience of minority Muslim communities expanded owing to the vision and support of Patricia L. Rosenfield and Hillary S. Wiesner from Carnegie Corporation. Among the scholars I met from Southeast Asia, two—the late Alber Husin (to whom the manifesto is dedicated) and Jowel Canuday—came to a conference on Muslim cosmopolitanism I was able to convene in Doha in December 2010, thanks to the generosity of Sheikha Al Mayassa Al Thani, then head of the Qatar Museum Authority, who had invited miriam cooke (my spouse) and me to be scholars in residence at the Museum of Islamic Art. My thanks are due not just to Sheikha Al Mayassa Al Thani but also to others who attended and contributed to that conference: Walter Mignolo, Kevin W. Fogg, Sita Hidayah, Dereje Feyissa, Jonathan Cross, Afyare Abdi Elmi, Anthony Shenoda, Andrew Simon, Amira Sonbol, Sulayman Khalaf, Mohammed Ali Abdalla, and, of course, miriam cooke. miriam has also provided me with countless hours of proofreading and correcting the manuscript, just as she joined me in the lunch conversation of 2019 at the University of Exeter, recounted in the Preamble. Other colleagues at Exeter enhanced the horizons of my work: Robert Gleave, Sajjad Rizvi, Ian Netton, William Gallois, Istvan Kristo-Nagy, Mustafa Baig, Emily Selove, and Rasheed El-Anany, while back in North Carolina, other scholars added to the chorus of support: Anne Allison and Charles Piot, with spirited commentary, Michelle Lamprakos and Steven Kramer, by close reading, and Leela and Baba Prasad as audacious critics. I am also indebted to the Abdullah S. Kamel Center for the Study of Islamic Law and Civilization at Yale Law School for hosting a conference marking the 50th anniversary of Hodgson's demise. Titled "Marshall Hodgson and the Contested Idea of a Discernible Islamic Civilization" it convened on November 9, 2018 and included along with myself these participants: Richard Bulliet, Richard M. Eaton, Wael Hallaq, Hedayat Haikal, David Nirenberg, Ahmed El-Shamsy, Nile Green, Carol Hillenbrand, Kevin van Bladel, and Frank Griffel. Anthony T. Kronman, Owen Fiss, and Bradley Hayes made the event sizzle, and I begin the Preamble with reflections that they

Acknowledgments

inspired, though neither they nor any of the above-mentioned supporters are responsible for the case I make, and the arguments I advance, for an Islamicate Cosmopolitan Spirit. I am finally indebted to the three outside reviewers for Wiley-Blackwell, all of whom sharpened the tone and expanded the scope of my manifesto, while miriam cooke added her voice to theirs in foregrounding my own voice throughout what follows.

Preamble

Why Islamicate, why now, why me? These three questions will occur to anyone who picks up this manifesto. They deserve a prompt answer, a brief self-disclosure.

Islamicate is a neologism for what pertains to Islam and Muslims. It was coined by the American historian Marshall Hodgson. Islamicate defines the arc of Islam beyond religious boundaries. It is at once a cultural and an ethical term. Though not devoid of religious tones, it registers them as subtle undertones rather than explicit dicta. Hodgson introduced this term in the 1960s but he died suddenly in 1968, his work unpublished. It was only 6 years later in 1974, thanks to the tireless labor of his colleague, Reuben Smith, that there appeared a posthumous publication titled *The Venture of Islam: Conscience and History in a World Civilization*. It consists of three volumes, published by the University of Chicago Press.

I never met Hodgson nor did I ever study at the University of Chicago. I had been in India when the book appeared, and I first read it in the summer of 1976 after my return to the United States. Enthralled, I began to teach all three volumes in a year-long Duke University undergraduate course titled "Islamic Civilization." I taught the course for more than three decades, till my retirement from Duke in 2011. Though many students were engaged by Hodgson, others found his mode of reasoning, as also his labored writing style, difficult to fathom. Yet even some of these dissidents later shared with me his profound influence on their world view and career choices.

A decade ago, I proposed to write a manifesto for Wiley-Blackwell on Muslim cosmopolitanism, but 4 years later in 2014 I was invited to contribute a reflection on *The Venture of Islam* and its author for the *LARB* (*Los Angeles Review of Books*), and began to explore not Muslim but rather Islamicate cosmopolitanism. I noted: "it involves not just Muslims but all those who are engaged by Muslim others. Islamicate pluralism has emerged, and deserves analysis, as the unexpected yet evident consequence of Hodgson's moral, cosmopolitan vision."[1] I discovered that more and more scholars were starting to engage with Hodgson, his methodology (hemispheric history), and his vocabulary (neologisms, including Islamicate, but also Islamdom, Nile-to-Oxus, Persianate, and Afro-Eurasian ecumene). The notion of Islamicate cosmopolitan became inescapable and compelling. In spring 2015, I gave a lecture at Duke's Franklin Humanities Institute titled: "Islamicate Cosmopolitan: A Past without a Future, or a Future still Unfolding?" In that lecture, I further explored the legacy of Hodgson's approach and his challenge to binary notions of Muslim identity and hackneyed surveys of Islamic history.[2]

At that time, I noted in many quarters a reluctance about the man, his mercurial career, and now his longer impact on world history. That reluctance was in full display when Yale Law School announced a further tribute to Hodgson, a 50-year retrospect in November 2018. I had been invited, along with eight other senior scholars, to present working papers on aspects of Hodgson. (Two commentators summarized four papers each in morning, then afternoon sessions, with a keynote address at noon.)[3] Some presenters were highly critical, especially of the neologism Islamicate and the key term civilization. But Hodgson also has his proponents, many of them outside the Euro-American academy, notably younger scholars. Since 2012 I have been teaching in Istanbul. Several of my students there, and also some colleagues, notably Ercüment Asil and Huricihan Islamoğlu, convinced me that more could and should be said in defense of Hodgson. Someone needed to explain the continuing value of his insights, not least his neologisms, for a new generation of scholars attuned to his civilizational vision, especially its ethical as well as analytic import. Why not me, and why not now?

And so, this book evolved as a different manifesto, with an accent on Islamicate/Persianate trajectories shaped by a common cosmopolitan spirit. Because the topic is deeply lettered, there are references that must be traced, acknowledged, lauded, or critiqued, but above all, framed in a manifesto on Islamicate, which is also cosmopolitan and which resonates as spirit. I will say more about Islamicate Cosmopolitan Spirit in the pages that follow, but this book would have been completed much earlier had the number of publications relating to the Persianate world, and Persianate elements in Islamicate history, not exploded during recent years. I deal with the major edited volumes in Chapter 5, but the one caveat I offer to the inquiring reader is: be alert to Persianate themes and evidence of a Persianate stratum of Islamicate influence, far beyond what I examine in the pages that follow. The answer to my 2015 question is now clear to me: Islamicate cosmopolitan persists, its future still unfolding.

Notes

1 See http://blog.lareviewofbooks.org/larb-channels/genius-denied-reclaimed-40-year-retrospect-marshall-g-s-hodgsons-venture-islam.
2 Available online at: https://humanitiesfutures.org/papers/islamicate-cosmopolitan-past-without-future-future-still-unfolding.
3 The full program with paper titles and presenters is provided at: https://law.yale.edu/yls-today/yale-law-school-events/marshall-hodgson-and-contested-idea-discernible-islamic-civilization.

Overview: A Manifesto in Three Words and Six Chapters

In the aftermath of the 2003 US invasion of Iraq, the blogger Riverbend observed: "What is civilization? It's not mobile phones, computers, skyscrapers, and McDonalds. It's having enough security in your own faith and culture to allow people the sanctity of theirs …"[1]

How do we define civilization as the deepest recognition of mutual and interactive sanctities? Riverbend's shibboleth is mine: finding the connection and fostering the opportunity to recognize, then engage seeming opposite, even hostile others who are no less human for being unlike us.

No global civilization can exclude Islam, but how to include it? The search for an inclusive civilizational ethos worthy of the name reached a tipping point for me in the United Kingdom last year. It was mid-February 2019. I was at the University of Exeter as a visiting scholar in residence. We had just completed a 2-hr lunchtime workshop. I got to pick the topic and the title for the talk. My title: "Islamicate Cosmopolitan?"

The title, posed as a question, was intended to be provocative. *What* is Islamicate? And *who* qualifies as an Islamicate cosmopolitan?

After an intense exchange that went beyond the usual lunch hour, we were about to disperse when a senior colleague asked: "So what?"

"So what?!" I rejoined, in surprise.

"You have made our lunch hour into two hours," he joked, adding "You have reflected on all the options and argued for a new tongue twister—Islamicate cosmopolitan. But do you really feel that this phrase is an epistemic turn worth pursuing? Where can one find a guide for the perplexed, some text illumining our understanding of both Islamicate and its coordinate term, cosmopolitan?"

This manifesto is my answer to my colleague's challenge. My motive is also my hope: to enliven each term with the other, Islamicate as cosmopolitan, cosmopolitan as Islamicate. But each needs a further referent, and so I am introducing a still broader trope: Islamicate Cosmopolitan Spirit, itself the entry way to civilizational options at once inclusive and enduring.

Islamicate Cosmopolitan Spirit

Since a manifesto is an extended general essay rather than a specialized monograph, I want to stress each word in my chosen topic: Islamicate Cosmopolitan Spirit. At the most basic level each connotes a surplus: Islamicate is more than Islamic or Muslim, Cosmopolitan is more than congenial or civil, and Spirit is more than subject or agent. Together Islamicate Cosmopolitan Spirit projects the presence of a tidal wave in world history that remains hidden for most, opaque for many, and misunderstood even by experts.

Each of these three key terms requires a brief history. But they also elicit a prior question about history itself: is historical revision desirable, even necessary? If so, is it possible without revising the categories or key terms in which history is framed?

For Islam, there is a need for revisionist terminology. I would argue that the need is even more urgent because "Islam" has become encumbered with misinterpretation in public discourse since 1979 and the Iranian revolution but even more since the terrorist attacks of 9/11 and two wars in largely Muslim countries: first Afghanistan, then Iraq. What must be foregrounded at the outset is stubborn resistance, from many quarters, to moving beyond "Islam" or "Muslim" in order to describe the 1,400-year experience that marked the birth, growth, and expansion of a 7th-century Arabian political-religious movement into a transregional presence. Islam did originate from Arabia but it quickly extended westward to Spain and eastward to China. Far from being Arab centered, the Islam movement redefined much of Africa and Asia, while itself being redefined by Africa and Asia, before impacting what became Western Europe and North America. The nagging question persists: what has been the surplus of value beyond Arab origins and Arabic language in its continued expansion and adaptation to multiple contexts in myriad cultures? In cultural studies, "Islamic music," "Islamic literature," and "Islamic art" persist as labels. In philosophical studies, "Islamic philosophy" continues to be invoked, while in historical studies one must look hard to find alternatives to "Islamic history." Even revisionists balk at changing their key terms, but I want to argue from the outset that unless that change is made, and unless it is consistently applied, there can be no revisionism worthy of the name. Old habits die slowly but die they must if a fresh vision is to emerge. A new day is dawning for understanding the long shadow of early 7th-century Arabia. The path will not be just through micro-analysis or regional studies but through meta-discourse, at the heart of which is salient and defensible key terms. A meta-discursive provocation is the goal of what follows.

What is Islamicate? Islamicate is neither a first nor a second but a third order of identity beyond "Muslim" and "Islamic," its two precursors, both crowded with religious valence. Despite its prevalence, religion itself can become a veil rather than a catalyst for understanding broad historical movements. Neither "Muslim" nor "Islamic" because of their close association with "religion" can reveal the tapestry of culture and cultural networks, and without being revealed that tapestry remains occluded, undervalued, too often minimalized, or ignored.

"Muslim" marks a religious but also a social identity. In 2020 "Muslim" is the first order of identity for about 2 billion out of nearly 8 billion of the world's population. One can be a Muslim by birth or by decision. In Arabic there are no capital letters, yet in English one is able to distinguish between two kinds of Muslim/ muslim, one capitalized, the other not. In a revisionist vocabulary one should be able to note the distinction. Who is a muslim with a small "m"? Who is a Muslim with a capital "M"? In the latter case, to be Muslim is to avow Islam as a pious, practicing individual but one can also be muslim, in the lower case, by association as the member of a collective, whether family, country, region, or the globe, that has been marked by Islam without professing or practicing Islam. Non-Muslims, of course, can also be muslims. If I were a thoroughgoing revisionist, I would distinguish between *both* categories in what follows, but since English does not yield to such lexical subtleties without constant bracketing in inverted commas, that endeavor would distract from my major purpose: to underscore the need for an alternative to religious monikers, both "Islamic" and "Muslim." In what follows, I will refer to Muslim, even though "muslim" remains an undertone of Muslim for those who are non-Muslim but also for many who may be neither devout nor observant as Muslims yet are routinely assumed to be cradle-to-grave believers in Allah as God, Muhammad as His last prophet, and the Qur'an as the final revelation for humankind.

Equally valuable but also ambivalent is "Islamic." Reflexively, "Islamic" serves as the second order of identity for one who is Muslim. To be Muslim is to connect with Islam across centuries and borders, always acknowledging the norms and values linked to Islamic texts, leaders, and institutions. Yet the intrusion of English and the now commonplace usage of "Islamist" with a violent connotation makes it imperative to rethink the larger contour of Islamicate history. Over 1,400 years Islam has often been portrayed with negative stereotypes, from the medieval Crusades to modern colonialism but added to that multiply layered identity of Muslim/Islamic is the recent history of Islam, often defined by headlines of violence during the past half-century. The 1970s were marked by two eruptions: the Iranian Revolution (February 1979), followed by the Soviet invasion of Afghanistan (December 1979). These two events inaugurated a series of wars and crises that highlight Muslims and Islam as, in Elaine Sciolino's phrase, "the Green menace," replacing the disappearing (but now reappearing) "Red menace," that is, the Soviet Union or Greater Russia.

While I oppose the contemporary or presentist bias, I also cannot ignore its pervasive influence. It produces a stigma, the stigma attached to Islam and, by extension, Muslims—too often riffed as Islamists—in 21st-century Euro-America. Unavoidable is the gaze of global media that defines events and actors through soundbites and images, usually negative. With the ubiquitous instant info world that we now take for granted, where tweets often count more than books, newspapers, or even television, one must ask: can Islam ever be free of the weaponizing proclivity of terror images? There are more than 1 billion Muslims worldwide, and few have anything to do with terror, yet if every Muslim is deemed a potential Islamist, can Islam itself be retained as a category of analysis without further exceptionalizing, minoritizing, and negativizing Muslims? For "Muslim" cosmopolitanism to work, it must extract the category "Islam" from the baggage it has acquired through daily, media saturation with negative images of Arab/Muslim/Islamic. If bad or violent, "Muslims" will appear in headlines, TV news, and tweets, but if good or cosmopolitan, they are relegated to the bylines or omitted, not just from essays and articles but also by visual media.

I would like to make the case for exceptions. They do exist, but their very paucity, and the reason for their paucity, underscore how "negative" Islamic/Muslim have become as labels in 21st-century America. Beyond Muhammad Ali, a sports hero to all, and Kareem Abd al-Jabbar, a basketball superstar, there are two Muslima Americans who were recently elected to the U.S. House of Representatives: Rashida Tlaib from Michigan and Ilhan Omar from neighboring Minnesota. I applaud these women, as do many other Americans who are alert to a pluralist, progressive public square of debate and compromise but above all representation and advocacy. Yet these two Midwestern Muslima pioneers have been critiqued as well as lauded, by Muslims as by non-Muslims. More than mere politicians, they, unlike their non-

Muslim counterparts, are seen to carry the weight of co-religionists with whom they share little other than the label "Muslim."[2]

Why Islamicate? Because a New Vocabulary Is Needed

The very act of defending Islam detracts from the deeper layers of cultural complexity that affect the domain where Islam has been introduced and Muslims are prevalent, either as majority or minority citizens. I move beyond the impasse it creates. I attempt to retrieve the larger contour of global history marked by Islam and Muslims. Throughout this manifesto I recuperate "Islam" and "Muslim" by locating both in a third referent, Islamicate. I argue that one cannot simply refute the notion that Islam is violent, or that Muslims are *all* Islamists; one must have a counternarrative that infuses the longer trajectory of Islam with elements that do not erase violence but instead reduce its dominance as the sole or main activity of Muslim subjects.

Let me give an instance of how difficult it is when even scholars ignore the role that "violence" plays in shaping every effort to address "Islam" or evaluate "Muslims." The late Shahab Ahmed, a skilled interpreter of Muslim intellectual history, tried to recuperate Islam from violence by generalizing the scope of Islam and minimizing its violent subset. Ahmed argued that in all instances, no matter the activity or its register, only "Islamic" satisfies the requirements of being Muslim or being linked to Islam. He wrote his own manifesto, in the form of an extended dialogue with prior scholars on Islam and Islamic history. He justifies his preference for Islam over Islamicate as follows:

> As long as the Muslim actor is making his act of violence meaningful to himself in terms of Islam … then it is appropriate and meaningful to speak of that act of violence as Islamic violence. The point of the designation is not that Islam *causes* this violence; rather

it is that the violence is made meaningful by the act or in terms of Islam ... One Muslim may disagree with another Muslim over whether his mode of meaning-making is legitimate—that is to say, whether it is *coherent* with its source—and may on those terms of incoherence deem the professed Muslim actor a non-Muslim, but the point is whether the actor makes the act meaningful for himself in terms of Islam.[3]

But what is the substantive basis of Islam apart from individual agency? Once we posit that there is no Islam beyond what individual Muslims say it is, then all who claim to speak on behalf of Islam as genuine, observant Muslims are correct, even when they differ. There are no "bad" Muslims and there is no "incorrect" Islam. That reductionism needs to be avoided but it can only be avoided if we use "religious labels" with attention to their historical context. To be Islamic in the 21st century, as in the 11th century, means more than being a believer in Allah, and a follower of Muhammad. But what is the extra element beyond the religious label, however re-fined and redefined? One has to look at other avenues of meaning, other vistas of hope in the long history of what I prefer to call Islamicate civilization. I argue in this manifesto that one needs to suspend the religious labeling of everyone Muslim, or mislabeling of Muslim as Islamist, in order to find that other sphere of origin and influence. Like Hodgson, I call that larger element "Islamicate" because it draws on Muslim/Islamic antecedents but out of an expansive reservoir of human experience and expression that exceeds religion. It is not secular but centripetal, always attracting a mixture of elements that are both religious and cultural.

• Islamicate is at once social and political, aesthetic and literary yet always in flux. According to one of its recent, eloquent definitions, "Islamicate = the hybrid trace rather than pure presence or absence of Islam."[4] Islamicate traces can be antecedent or subsequent,[5] before or after "Islam," but in every instance they exceed objective analysis since they are in-between markers, reflecting gray rather than black and white, ambiguity and flexibility rather than fixity, rigidity, or "objectivity." As one frequent traveller to many Muslim domains, Asian and African, has noted: "Islamicate = Islam filtered in diverse contexts, reflecting synergy between Muslims and non-Muslims apart from creedal or ritual allegiances."[6] Whether Islam filtered or Islam as hybrid trace, "Islamicate" exceeds binary categories or narrow norms of identity. It inflects fuzzy or *barzakh* logic, as I will explain below.

Why Cosmopolitan? Because it Values Bi-location in Two Worlds

Islamicate both complements and qualifies cosmopolitan because "cosmopolitan," like Islamicate, is a category in flux. It has often been linked to Europe or the European enlightenment as an encompassing expression of mobility, generosity, and tolerance, yet cosmopolitan is broader than Europe, having an ecumenical reach that literally encompasses the Afro-Eurasian ecumene; that is, the inhabited world as it was known for more than two millennia.[7] There are so many competing definitions of cosmopolitanism that it seems preferable to list some of these scholars before declaring which I choose to present and defend in this manifesto. All are acknowledged leaders in social scientific engagement with cosmopolitanism, and since one collected volume has included their analyses, I list six options from Vertovec and Cohen in order to highlight the enigma they collectively pose:

- Cosmopolitanism may be a cultural, and cognitive, orientation, specifically, "the ability to stand outside a singular location (the location of one's birth, land, upbringing, conversion) and to mediate traditions."[8]
- But cosmopolitanism may also be the social experience of difference without threat, above all, in urban locations, where

one moves through offices or zones of the city "reconciling alterity and rigidity, or alterity and rationality, with a notion of temporary identification."[9]

- Cosmopolitanism may also not be individual but collective, an awareness oriented toward an agonistic democratic process, one that involves communities who find themselves "in that open space that requires a kind of vernacular cosmopolitanism." Cosmopolitanism is then not about an individual life style nor a universalist morality nor global political institutions, but rather it is about the "vision of a cosmo-*polis*, a global community of citizens."[10]

- More specifically, cosmopolitanism might project an inclusive democratic strategy. While cosmopolitanism is presumed to be inherently urban, elitist, and consumerist, might it not also involve redefining social solidarities to engender mutual commitment and responsibility from the greatest number of citizens? In this case, "cosmopolitan democracy depends on finding ways to relate diverse solidarities to each other rather than trying to overcome them."[11] Implicit in all the above is what has been openly stated by other social scientists: the cosmopolitan has to engage nationalism, and so for two other theorists, it is not just citizenship but nationalism, as also redefining national identity as a modern reflex of global capitalism, that must be at the core of any cosmopolitan project. Yet nationalism itself is not a consistent or constant analytical referent; it reflects at least two tangents of cosmopolitan sensibility.

- Cosmopolitanism must be "modern" and national and that means: Option One. "There is no opposition between cosmopolitanism and nationalism. They emerged together, and they belong together in the context of an emerging capitalist world-system."[12] Or else: Cosmopolitanism must be modern and "global" and that means: Option Two. Cosmopolitanism is simply globalism writ large, that is to say, "the self-definition and public reflexivity of transnational ways of life and situations, not only at the top but also at the bottom and in the middle of an emerging society of world citizens."[13] Despite their seeming disagreement, Options One and Two converge in their focus on the necessity of national markers: every cosmopolitan must have a national identity, but at same time s/he needs to be committed to working against exclusive forms of national, ethnic, or local identity. What is presupposed and promoted is the vision of a cosmopolis, a global community of like-minded citizens, and that runs the risk of alienating or subjugating minorities, as Hannah Arendt has argued. It is precisely a resolute, if often unacknowledged, nationalist spirit that made cosmopolitanism impossible because it created the nation in terms of what it is not, that is, newly minted minorities without the rights of the majority. Cosmopolitanism becomes a form of neo-tribalism for elites only, caught between an imperial past and a totalitarian headwind.[14] Suffusing all these definitional efforts is the thrust of a cosmopolitan ethos, and because it is an aspiration, like every ethical norm, it is more readily sensed in its adjectival than in its nominal form; the *-ism* suggests an ideological closure that the adjective resists. In the interest of openness, I speak of Islamicate cosmopolitan, not Islamicate cosmopolitanism. The frame in which I locate each Islamicate Cosmopolitan Spirit is the historical trajectory and capacious context of Islamicate civilization.

Why Civilization? Because Every Cosmopolitan Has Civilizational Roots

While there are many elements to Islamicate cosmopolitan, its central inescapable core is an interactive, civilizational framework. "Civilization" as a category has been, and will continue to be, disputed, but what is beyond dispute is the linking of civilization with civility and so with polis or city. Without civilization, civility, and cities there would be no cosmopolitan ethos, whether Islamicate, Persianate, Italianate, or Christianate.[15] Herein lies a tension, between the verticality of "the cosmos," and the horizontal rootedness of "the polis." It is a tension to be explored below, but one should underscore that civility requires belonging to some polis or city place, and without that belonging there could not be the longing to make the world the larger—indeed, the largest—place of belonging.

The implications of the cosmopolitan turn augur a new paradigm dating back a mere 30 years.[16] The paradigm meanders within and across the Afro-Asian ecumene, with huge implications for understanding Islamicate cosmopolitan. The first, critical link is historical. Islamicate did not originate with the coming of Islam; it had deep roots in Irano-Semitic social and institutional patterns. In other words, the traces of Islamicate cosmopolitan preceded the historical advent of Islam. A prominent sociologist, Armando Salvatore, explains the historical trajectory as follows:

> On the one hand, Islamicate civilization revealed a strong rooting within the Irano-Semitic cultural world. On the other, by virtue of the articulation of Islam itself as a religious tradition that sealed the chain of Semitic prophecy while also integrating the rich and complex heritage of Persianate culture, it was particularly porous to inter-civilizational exchange. This is why Islam quickly acquired a uniquely expansive potential in cultural, as well as political, terms.[17]

By itself Islam does not account for the cultural legacy of Iran, the Persianate strand that pervades, and also redefines, Islamicate civilization, above all in the magisterial guise of spirit. There is a constant tension as well as interactive creativity between the Irano-Semitic, and also the Perso-Arabic, and then the Persianate-Islamicate folds of world history. Persianate is a direct consequence of Islamicate developments, even as it becomes the embodiment of Islamicate taste and influence through much of Central, South, and South-east Asia, including the Indian Ocean. It is not the dominance of one over the other but the continuous interaction of Persianate with Islamicate that expands the role of moral imagination and cultural productivity in Muslim-dominant regions of the Afro-Eurasian ecumene.

Why Spirit? Because Islamicate Cosmopolitan is Fluid and Restless

The rapid spread of Islam in the 7th century compelled its conquering forces to adapt to multiple civilizations as far west as Spain and as far east as China. Islamicate civilization from the outset evinces a cosmopolitan ethos marked by the two key traits of longing and belonging. The belonging is always a reflex of power, the privilege of literacy and mobility but also the benefits of imperial patronage. All premodern Islamicate cosmopolitans benefited from hierarchical social-political structures. Yet that benefit did not limit their horizons, for allied with belonging was longing, the longing for something more, a surplus of benefit to humankind beyond their immediate time/space frame.

It is that surplus of benefit, which is also a higher level of meaning, that requires a further adjective as qualifier. To explore and try to explain Islamicate cosmopolitan one must recognize not just its origins but also its aspiration. There was never a fixed horizon. It was always an elan, a *spirit*, and cosmopolitans themselves, whatever their time/space belonging, remain *spirited* agents of change, delineated by their period and place in the canvas of human history but not delimited in their imagination or aspiration for a humane world order feels too generalized. To corral them as parochial, territorial, or ideological is to deny them their own deepest longing: to project beyond the limits of their loyalties to affirm others whatever their loyalties. They are less Islamicate cosmopolitan "national" subjects than aspiring agents of a multilingual, transnational Islamicate Cosmopolitan Spirit, both Persian and Arab, both Iranian and Semitic, heirs to others, harbingers of many others.

There are many who qualify as Islamicate cosmopolitan spirits through affirming this aspiration. One notable modern exemplar appears in the aftermath of the 2003 U.S. invasion of Iraq. Quoted above was the blogger Riverbend: "what is civilization? It's not mobile phones, computers, skyscrapers, and McDonalds; It's having enough security in your own faith and culture to allow people the sanctity of theirs …" One can trace a direct line from Diogenes, the Greek orator, who proclaimed: "I am a citizen of the world," and his neighbour—not in time but in outlook—Riverbend. Crucially, it is important to note where in the world one claims to be a citizen. For Riverbend, unlike Diogenes, it was in the midst of a warzone, with material, social, and cultural destruction at a level that made the plea for cosmopolitan thinking a rescue shibboleth rather than a boutique advertisement. The distance from Martha Nussbaum's notion of world citizenry is evident, and of course there are multiple detractors from *any* cosmopolitan identity. One need look no further than the opinion page of *The New York Times*, where Ross Douthat depicted what he called "the myth of cosmopolitanism" as subsuming others into "a meritocratic order that transforms difference into similarity, by plucking the best and brightest from everywhere and homogenizing them into the peculiar species that we call 'global citizens.'"[18] This is, of course, a caricature of cosmopolitan longing and belonging, depicted above, and while there are "Muslims" in this club, they do not reflect the Islamicate Cosmopolitan Spirit.

Islamicate Cosmopolitan Spirit as Fuzzy or *Barzakh* Logic

And that aspiration brings to the fore the second major impetus for this manifesto: what makes an Islamicate cosmopolitan *spirit* (rather than visible form or invisible substance) is fuzzy logic. Fuzzy logic as a category is itself recent. Devised little more than half a century ago by an Azeri scientist who had migrated to the United States, it has now branched into a broader linguistic strategy that helps to define cosmopolitan tensions generally and Islamicate cosmopolitan in particular. Fuzzy logic is often heralded as self-critical, even ironic, so it is a further, fitting irony that fuzzy logic becomes the pillar of Islamicate Cosmopolitan Spirit since the founder of fuzzy logic, Lotfi Zadeh, is himself an Islamicate cosmopolitan, even though he himself has yet to emerge in the larger universe of constructive rethinking of the key terms he helped to formulate. As early as a 1965 article he had introduced fuzzy sets but it was the subsequent 1975 article that makes the case for their implementation in cosmopolitan reflection. His language is dense but its appeal evocative. "The concept of a linguistic variable," argues Lotfi Zadeh, "provides a means of approximate characterization of phenomena which are too complex or too ill-defined to be amenable to description in conventional quantitative terms. In particular, treating ZFuth as a linguistic variable with values such as true, very true, completely true, not very true, untrue, etc., leads to what is called fuzzy logic. By providing a basis for approximate reasoning, that is, a mode of reasoning which is not exact nor very inexact, such logic may offer a more realistic framework for human reasoning than the traditional two-valued logic."[19]

Of course, ZFuth is itself a nonsensical term introduced to make the point that conventional language, like conventional numbers ("conventional quantitative terms"), has to be approached with a new kind of reasoning beyond Aristotelian bivalent logic ("traditional two-valued logic").

If fuzzy sets are the exemplars of fuzzy logic, that is "collections of information whose boundaries were vague or imprecise,"[20] then all cosmopolitan theories are sets of information at once discrete in their common subject yet unbounded in their actual formation and historical emergence. They are always marked by their "spirit," that is, by a commitment to explore the limits of what is possible, so that "spirit" does not merely connote the life force, but also the essential human trait manifest as consciousness, discernment, and, above all, moral motivation—to do not just what is right but what is best, not just for oneself but for all others, a combination of agonism and altruism.

The benefit of the fuzzy logic approach to Islamicate Cosmopolitan Spirit is what some theorists have labeled heterology: the other as a foundational principle of the self.[21] In expanding Islamic to Islamicate, one must consider not just the Other, but multiple others, those others that preceded and informed Islam. One must revisit and revalue all the resources on which Muslim actors—from artists to traders to rulers to philosophers—drew in rethinking the nature of Islamic pursuits through the lens of those others. The very boundaries of Islamicate civilization, as also Islamicate Cosmopolitan Spirit, become fungible, extending back to 500 CE, in considering Byzantine and Sasanian but also Ethiopian antecedents.[22] And the further teleological reach of Islamicate civilization, and so its cosmopolitan ethos, is not just the 18th century. Instead of ending with the advent of the Great Western Transmutation,[23] it lingers, projecting a flash point, or set of points across Africa and Asia, spaces that can still summon what one scholar calls islands of life/light in the midst of what seems to be a binary world of North/South replacing East/West.[24]

And so, to answer my colleague from the University of Exeter, whose query spurred me to clarify my intent, let me close with a brief two-part summary of why I have pursued the Islamicate Cosmopolitan Spirit challenge and am now writing this manifesto.

First are the new forays and the several arguments for rethinking world history outside the West while also not ignoring the West. Let us label that tangent: the demands of world history.

Coupled with the demands of world history is the need for revisionist vocabulary and also attention to the rules of fuzzy logic. My central premise: not to accept binary divisions but to look for in-between spaces, alternative players, and dimly lit options that herald a new methodology. Let us call that methodology: the rules of fuzzy logic.

Let me pause and make a detour at the outset. For those to whom "fuzzy logic" is itself too fuzzy, there is an alternative: *barzakh* logic. Neither dualistic nor binary but triadic, *barzakh* logic both affirms and denies, while neither affirming nor denying. I call it *barzakh* logic because, like fuzzy logic, it requires its practitioners to be grounded in science, like Wittgenstein, a mathematician–engineer turned linguistic philosopher. To see the limits of science one must first know its protocols. A theorist does not eliminate science but rather tries to recover the ground preceding and undergirding all true science, as did Bacon but also Pascal and later Polanyi and Peirce. *Barzakh* logic, like fuzzy logic, does not destroy or deny reason, but instead probes its frontiers, which are internal and sentient as much as external and cognitive.

Barzakh itself is a Persian word found in the Qur'an (Q 23:99–100, Q 25:53, and Q 55:19–20). At its simplest, the *barzakh* evokes the division between this life and the next, between our present life in this world and a future life beyond knowing, but *barzakh* also refers to the divide between salt and fresh water, found in some oceans and rivers. And so *barzakh* is at once barrier and bridge. Like fuzzy logic, it moves beyond the binary dualism, either/or, but unlike fuzzy logic, it confirms a dyad, both/and as well as neither/nor. *Barzakh* might be defined as interactive, uninterrupted connection, linking two things—whether two cosmic realms or two bodies of water or two key terms—without reducing or diluting either. Nor can the *barzakh* itself be reduced: it cannot be triangulated to produce yet another form of abstractionism. If *barzakh* logic or its companion, fuzzy logic, is to apply, it requires constant vigilance against the reflex to rely on binary categories and the ontology they both presume and promote.[25]

And so, we begin with these twin exigencies, at once declarations and guideposts, mandates and shibboleths, for all that follows: (a) world history must be revised, and (b) the rules of fuzzy or *barzakh* logic must apply. Together, a world history revised in tandem with fuzzy or *barzakh* logic forms the basis for an enduring Islamicate Cosmopolitan Spirit.

Notes

1   From a blog titled "Civilization," posted on Tuesday, October 21, 2003. http://riverbendblog.blogspot.com/2003/10 (accessed May 22, 2020).
2   For the Saudi critique of both women, see the scorching essay by Hamid Dabashi, "Why Saudi Arabia hates Muslim women in the US Congress," January 2019 published online at https://www.aljazeera.

com/indepth/opinion/saudi-arabia-hates-muslim-women-congress-190126055438087.html. I have also written extensively on the misuse of violence as a category besmirching all Muslims across time and place, especially in Bruce B. Lawrence, "Muslim Engagement with Injustice and Violence" in Mark Juergensmeyer, Margo Kitts, and Michael Jerryson, eds., *The Oxford Handbook of Religion and Violence* (New York, NY: Oxford University Press, 2013): 126–152.

3   Shahab Ahmed, *What is Islam? The Importance of Being Islamic* (Princeton, NJ: Princeton University Press, 2016): 452.

4   Srinivas Aravamudan, "East–West Fiction as World Literature: the Hayy Problem Reconfigured," *Eighteenth-Century Studies* 47(2) (2014), 198. I am indebted to Aravamudan for many stimulating discussions on Islamicate as a cosmopolitan qualifier across time and space, in Europe and Asia, in the 11th, 18th, and now 21st centuries. For a fuller reference to Aravamudan, as also to the complicated genealogy of (non)use of Islamicate cosmopolitan, see my 2014 intervention at https://humanitiesfutures.org/papers/islamicate-cosmopolitan-past-without-future-future-still-unfolding (accessed February 15, 2021).

5   Let me be clear: what comes "before" Islam is also deemed Islamicate, only in retrospect. Aristotelian philosophy, like Byzantine architecture, had elements of reciprocity with Islamic norms and values, and so became Islamicate continuously, often seamlessly, after the 7th–8th and successive centuries.

6   Pru Lambert during a conversation in London, fall 2014.

7   For the term Afro-Eurasian ecumene, see Marshall G.S. Hodgson, *The Venture of Islam: Conscience and History in a World Civilization*, vol. 1 (Chicago, IL: University of Chicago Press, 1974): 173–174, where Hodgson states his preference for "*oikoumene*" over "*ecumene*," since the latter for him retains the adjectival shadow of "ecumenical." On this point, I disagree with Hodgson since ecumene retains a rigorously historical rather than purely theological nuance. Even in disagreeing with him, however, I, along with other revisionist historians, remain indebted to his bold forays into the global as well as moral trajectories of civilizational analysis.

8   David Held in Steven Vertovec and Robin Cohen, eds., *Conceiving Cosmopolitanism: Theory, Context, and Practice* (New York, NY: Oxford University Press, 2002): 58.

9   Richard Sennett in Steven Vertovec and Robin Cohen, eds., *Conceiving Cosmopolitanism: Theory, Context, and Practice* (New York, NY: Oxford University Press, 2002): 44–45.

10 Roger Baubock in Steven Vertovec and Robin Cohen, eds., *Conceiving Cosmopolitanism: Theory, Context, and Practice* (New York, NY: Oxford University Press, 2002): 111.

11 Craig Calhoun in Steven Vertovec and Robin Cohen, eds., *Conceiving Cosmopolitanism: Theory, Context, and Practice* (New York, NY: Oxford University Press, 2002): 108.

12 Peter van der Veer in Steven Vertovec and Robin Cohen, eds., *Conceiving Cosmopolitanism: Theory, Context, and Practice* (New York, NY: Oxford University Press, 2002): 178.

13 Ulrich Beck in in Steven Vertovec and Robin Cohen, eds., *Conceiving Cosmopolitanism: Theory, Context, and Practice* (New York, NY: Oxford University Press, 2002): 81, citing Robertson (1992), Albrow (1996), and Nassehi (1998).

14 The debate augured by Arendt is intense and also complex. For an engaged view of its historical trajectory, with special emphasis on the relation of imperial to totalitarian currents of change, see the insightful 2012 essay of a Turkish academic, Dr. M. Cagri Inceoglu, "Arendt's Critique of the Nation-State in *The Origins of Totalitarianism*," available online at https://dergipark.org.tr/tr/download/article-file/179189 (accessed February 15, 2021).

15 Both Italianate and Christianate have their own genealogy. Matthew Melvin-Koushki has contrasted Persian Islamicate with Latin Christianate. "Imperial grimoires—that is, manuals on various forms of magic and divination written for or commissioned by royal readers—also record the religiocultural and institutional divergences that so distinguish the Islamicate and especially Persianate experience of early modernity from the Latin Christianate. Historians of books, of science and of empire must therefore finally overcome the eurocentrism and occultophobia still endemic in these fields, and cease judging Islamicate imperial occultism by Christianate standards, or simply writing it out of history altogether." M. Melvin-Koushki, "How to Rule the World: Occult-Scientific Manuals of the Early Modern Persian Cosmopolis," *Journal of Persianate Studies* 11(2) (2018), 140–154; summary.

16   Martha Nussbaum, "Patriotism and Cosmopolitanism," *Boston Review* (October, 1994) spurred others to applaud and emulate, but also to decry and attack her. She herself changed positions over time, as evidenced by her recent, *The Cosmopolitan Tradition: A Noble but Flawed Ideal* (New Haven, CT: Harvard University Press, 2019). For the cosmopolitan turn in the social sciences, see Ulrich Beck and Edgar Grande, "Varieties of Second Modernity: The Cosmopolitan Turn in Social and Political Theory and Research," *British Journal of Sociology* 61(3) (2010), 409–443.

17   Armando Salvatore, *The Sociology of Islam: Knowledge, Power and Civility* (Oxford: Wiley-Blackwell, 2016): 29. Later, Salvatore reiterates and endorses the cosmopolitan nature of Islamicate civilization: "Hodgson thought that Islam brought to a new and particularly powerful synthesis the cosmopolitan and largely egalitarian orientation of the Irano-Semitic traditions" (p. 31). In what follows I demur only in suggesting that the egalitarian orientation was masked, or rather sublated, by hierarchical structures of reciprocity in court culture and beyond. See especially discussion throughout the book on *taskhir* and *adab*.

18   Ross Douthat, "The Myth of Cosmopolitanism," *The New York Times, Sunday Review* (July 2, 2016).

19   Lotfi Zadeh, "The Concept of a Linguistic Variable and Its Application to Approximate Reasoning," *Information Sciences* 8(3) (1975), 199–249.

20   Lotfi Zadeh, "Fuzzy Sets," *Information and Control* 8/3 (1965), 338–353. One of Zadeh's many admirers has described the implications of his thesis as follows: "the central thesis is that everything is a matter of degree. The world is grey, not black-and-white. But Western scientists and philosophers have refused to face up to this fact; they persist in describing the grey world in black-and-white language." Their doing so is what the author calls the "mismatch problem," a problem rooted in the uncritical acceptance of two-valued logic—"binary faith." Binary logic sacrifices accuracy for simplicity. Bivalence is a rounding off that works fine at extremes but fails everywhere else. Indeed, the core principles of bivalent logic—the Law of Excluded Middle and the Principle of Non-Contradiction—are merely limiting cases of a more proper multi-valued logic (B. Kosko and

M. Toms, *Fuzzy Thinking: The New Science of Fuzzy Logic* (London: Harper Collins, 1993)). It is the same opposition to binary logic that characterizes *barzakh* logic, a parallel but variant form of nonbinary reasoning and argumentation.

21   I am thinking here of the Haitian anthropologist, Michel-Rolph Trouillot and his several works underscoring how "others" are created, then deployed for specific purposes. In depicting the Modern as heterology he observes: "As part of the geography of imagination that constantly recreates the West, modernity always required an Other and an Elsewhere. It was always plural, just like the West was always plural. This plurality is inherent in modernity itself, both structurally and historically." Michel-Rolph Trouillot, *Critically Modern: Alternatives, Alterities, Anthropologies* (Bloomington, IN: Indiana University Press, 2002): 224. I am also indebted to Walter Mignolo for conversations and communications, as well as his several published reflections, on this same subject. My sense of heterology is here inverted: the other, once acknowledged and recovered, becomes an extended, and productive, way of rethinking the self.

22   The pivotal importance of Ethiopia, despite its omission from most literature on Islamicate cosmopolitan (re)thinking, merits closer consideration. A collective initiative to correct this oversight can be found in Dereje Feyissa and Bruce B. Lawrence, "Muslims Renegotiating Marginality in Contemporary Ethiopia," *The Muslim World* 105 (July, 2014), 281–305.

23   This is the judgment of Hodgson in *The Venture of Islam*, vol. 3, reviewed but also qualified by Faisal Devji in chapter 9 "The Problem of Muslim Modernity", Edmund Burke and Robert J Mankin, eds., *Islam and World History* (Chicago, IL: University of Chicago Press, 2018), especially pp. 147–162.

24   William Gallois, "Al-Andalusi Cosmopolitanism in World History," but also the radiant book, Allen F. Roberts and Mary N. Roberts, *A Saint in the City: Sufi Arts of Urban Senegal* (Los Angeles, CA: University of California Press, 2003), heralding the labor and the legacy of Ahmadu Bamba in modern-day Senegal. I am indebted to Gallois both for this link and also his generosity of spirit in engaging

the notion of Islamicate cosmopolitan as a living, undying spirit animating both Muslims and non-Muslims in the 21st century.

25   A brief genealogy to *barzakh* logic would begin less than two decades ago. Its pioneer was Taieb Belghazi, "The Mediterranean(s), Barzakh, Event" in T. Belghazi and L.Haddad, eds., *Global/Local Cultures and Sustainable Development* (Rabat: Publications of the Faculty of Letters and Human Sciences, 2001): 217–236. More recently, it has been applied to the Arab/Persian Gulf in miriam cooke, *Tribal Modern: Branding New Nations in the Arab Gulf* (Berkeley, CA: University of California Press, 2014), where one reviewer noted that "cooke exquisitely captures the civilizational *barzakh* of the Arab Gulf states—the generative space connecting/disconnecting, mixing/separating 'the tribal' and 'the modern.'" For my own development of *barzakh* logic, with reference to the Andalusian philosopher-mystic, Muhyiddin ibn 'Arabi, see Bruce B. Lawrence, *Who is Allah?* (Chapel Hill, NC: University of North Carolina Press, 2015): 40–45.

1

Tracing Islamicate Cosmopolitan Spirit Across Time and Space

To look at Islamicate civilization is to face the choice of where and when to look but it also requires one to invoke fuzzy or *bar-zakh* logic at the outset. There is no great divide between East and West or between Islam and its political–religious rivals, whether in the premodern or the modern world. Many are the historians who have labored to point out that civilizational study is predicated on "gray" not black and white visions of the past, and multiple, local understandings of civilizational actors, events, institutions, and legacies.

In short, cosmopolitan studies, like civilizational studies with which it is allied and on which it must be modeled, requires decentering the West and reappropriating the "rest" for a deeper, truer sense of what is genuinely world history.

In that quest for a revisionist world history—or what one scholar has framed "a world history worthy of the name"[1]—Marshall Hodgson occupies a special place. His legacy has to be reviewed to understand how one builds on the edifice he proposed in order to trace the enduring influence of Islamicate Cosmopolitan Spirit (ICS).

Hodgson begins not with the premodern but with the modern world. He asks of himself the tough question all of us must ask: not what is Western but what is the force of "Western" as a descriptor

Islamicate Cosmopolitan Spirit, First Edition. Bruce B. Lawrence.
© 2021 Bruce B. Lawrence. Published 2021 by John Wiley & Sons, Ltd.

in the numerous theoretical studies on modernity? At the same time, he launches a thorough, all-out attack on Weberian notions of calculative rationalism. He challenges Weberian assumptions in offering a prognosis for transformation on a different calculus than others have made. As a world historian,[2] the arguments he makes for transformation apply to a broad spectrum of humankind. Religion looms as the catalyst for hopeful change, and for genuine transformation, in the future, but does religion assist or impede the modernization process?

I contest the assumption that only modernization finally works, and that religions must be judged good or bad by how congruent or dissonant they are with forces, structures, and goals of modernization. I prefer to stand this question on its head, suggesting that modernization is neither monolithic nor inevitable. It is not monolithic because it did not impact on all parts of Euro-America with equal success. Nor is it inevitable since it was a concatenation of circumstances rather than any single cluster of ideal traits or the convergence of such traits with technical discoveries, all of which produced what Hodgson termed the Great Western Transmutation.

The Great Western Transmutation overlooked the key forces that had forged all the great civilizations of premodern history: individual initiative and cultural creativity. They remain the twin ideals for Hodgson that caused him to describe the most recent axial shift as the Great Western *Transmutation*. Great Western *Transmutation* invokes Jaspers' notion of axial shift covering not only centuries but millennia of historical variation, while also affirming Weber's insight into the distinctive character of modern European technicalism. But at the same time, Hodgson wanted to acknowledge the social achievements and cultural norms of non-Western societies, highlighting what they had deemed to be both creative and productive. And so, in his major essay on the ambiguous character of modernity, published over 50 years ago (1967), Hodgson drew attention not to Euro-American global dominance but to the downside of this dominance for the dominated or marginalized. Noting that "gradual diffusions had maintained parity among *Afro-Eurasian citied societies*," he lamented that "the Western Transmutation, once it got well under way, could neither be paralleled independently nor be borrowed wholesale. Yet it could not, in most cases, be escaped. The millennial parity of social power broke down, with results that were disastrous almost everywhere."[3]

The Intervention of Huricihan Islamoğlu

A Turkish socio-economic historian, who herself studied with Hodgson, Huricihan Islamoğlu has offered a brief recapitulation of his legacy that underscores yet again why and how Islamicate civilization matters. In a 2012 essay titled "Islamicate World Histories?" Islamoğlu rehearses then reassesses several approaches to Ottoman historiography before closing with this query: can we write world histories that are genuinely "world histories"?

> Our present history at least suggests that it is time to look beyond Western domination. A genuine rethinking of world history implies transcending the binaries of West and non-West, European center and non-European periphery, premodern and modern. It implies questioning the identification of modernity with the West, whereby institutions emerging from Western history represented universal attributes of modernity, merely imported or adopted or resisted by non-Westerners [...]
>
> Decades ago, Marshall Hodgson remarked that without the rich cumulation of institutional innovations in the Afro-Eurasian *oikoumene* – including those in the Islamicate lands of the Ottoman, Mughal and Safavid empires – the Western transmutation would have been "unthinkable." That transmutation was itself part of world historical processes, representing mostly an acceleration of these processes in the late eighteenth century, in such a way as to result in Western world domination.

And the problem that this acceleration and dominance pose for global comity is the same for her as for Hodgson. What was lost was a differential view of human progress.

> For Hodgson this [pre-eighteenth century] concerted effort to respond to changing conditions through institutional innovation – to find new ways of ordering production, property rights, commercial transactions, and state administration – represented the "unity of history." That view of unity implied that different regions shaped and contributed to the core content of history. Hence, it is important to ask, *how* did different societies meet the challenge of modern transformation, what institutional solutions did they produce? Crucially, *all* the regions throughout Eurasia have been involved in the historical processes of modern transformation.[4]

Subsequently Islamoğlu elaborated on her expansive view of global change by adding an accent on the metaphysical underpinning, the core moral imperative, that suffuses *The Venture of Islam*. At WOC-MES 2014 in Ankara, she observed that:

> Central to Hodgson's work was a sense of the moral significance of the history one wrote. Above all, Islam's ongoing venture has been the sisyphus-like struggle of its elites seeking institutionally innovative solutions to meet multiple historical challenges. This pursuit of a moral life, at once individual and collective, continued in larger polities of empires amidst unpredictabilities and chaos following the Mongol invasions. The cast of elites expanded. It extended to include bureaucrats, warriors, merchants, industrialists. At the same time the moral concern for a just societal order focused on ideas of government and statecraft that developed in Islamicate societies but exceeded the borders of Muslim majority empires. They were shared and transmuted to become part of larger streams of world history.[5]

And so, the Hodgsonian legacy—an open-ended vision of history, committed to justice—remains vital, not least because civilization, Islamicate civilization, demands fresh rethinking in the

4

contemporary era. It has to be reclaimed for those who advocate an ICS in their time and for like-minded moral visionaries. If Hodgson was a product of the Cold War, fighting the demons of Western exceptionalism and anti-Communism, we are today products of a new age of connectivity and global imaginaries, marked unequally by networks of solidarity and resistance. Where are equality and justice, not just as empty slogans but as institutional markers of collective hope?

Above all, it is the geography of an ICS that offers new horizons. The expanse of Islamicate societies extends to the Indian Ocean and Southeast Asia but also to Euro-America and Africa. Those of us who study Islam must identify and herald the new elites who challenge us with a fresh moral vision, an Islamicate cosmopolitan ethos that seeks to replace the current world (dis)order with a sustainable, and just, new order. These are the latest generation of ICS exemplars. Let us mark Huricihan Islamoğlu and Riverbend at the forefront. Nor is it a mere accident that two leading ICS advocates should be women, since Hodgson himself was an advocate for gender as well as social justice, far in advance of his time.[6]

There are three crucial elements from Hodgson and Islamoğlu that need to be stressed: elites, empires, and modernity. Each has its own valence; none can be ignored in tracing ICS over time and space.

First, lives of elites matter. The Sisyphus-like struggle of Muslim elites—bureaucrats, warriors, merchants, industrialists, and scholars—was to seek solutions to multiple historical challenges. Nonelites also matter but elites dominate the civilizational kaleidoscope etched over time and space, and they are the primary class to consider as exemplars of ICS, Islamicate Cosmopolitan Spirit.

Second, empires matter. Elites' pursuit of a moral life continued in empires before and after the Mongol invasions. New ideas of statecraft developed in Islamicate societies. They exceeded the borders of Muslim majority empires, becoming part of larger streams of world history, and so it is impossible to calculate who embodied ICS without reference to the institutions and practices, the norms and values that marked these empires.

5

Third, modernity matters—everywhere. The Great Western Transmutation shadowed the open-ended vision of history, with an accent on justice, that Hodgson evoked vividly and repeatedly. In volume three of *The Venture of Islam*, he seems to argue that Islamicate societies persist even if Islamicate civilization vanishes. One must review that judgment on the peripheries, especially the West African and Southeast Asian peripheries, of the extant Afro-Eurasian ecumene, but it is first necessary to estimate the emergence of Islam, and so an Islamicate Cosmopolitan Spirit, on the two wings of empire: India and Andalusia.

Notes

1 See below, Huricihan Islamoğlu, "Islamicate World Histories?" in Douglas Northrup, ed., *A Companion to World History* (Oxford: Wiley-Blackwell, 2012): chapter 30, 447–463. She begins the final section (457–460) with the further query: "Can We Write World Histories that are Genuinely World Histories?".

2 Edmund Burke III observed that Hodgson had an unpublished book-length work, "The Unity of World History," which remains unpublished, though the last three chapters of that liminal work were published as Part III of Marshall G.S. Hodgson, *Rethinking World History: Essays on Europe, Islam and World History* (Studies in Comparative World History) (E. Burke, ed.). (Cambridge: Cambridge University Press, 1993): xi and 247–299. Edmund Burke III and Robert Mankin, eds., *Islam and World History: The Ventures of Marshall Hodgson* (Chicago, IL: University of Chicago Press, 2018), dedicates Part One to "Hodgson and World History." It consists of four essays, by Michael Geyer, Katja Naumann, C.A. Bayly, and Pamela Crossley. Along with other revisionist historians, I am indebted to Burke for his decades-long dedication to popularizing and expanding the legacy of Hodgson as a world historian.

3 Burke/Hodgson (1993): 70–71. While Hodgson did not know Enrique Dussel, it is impossible to imagine that he would not have agreed with Dussel's insight that European modernity is itself

ambiguous, bifurcated rather than unified in its role as a modern colonial project. A leading Mexican philosopher and world historian, Enrique Dussel depicts not one but two major forms of modernity. Hispanic modernity or Modernity I was centered in Seville. It projected a mercantilist and monetary expansion of Portuguese—but even more, Spanish—influence that included missionary projects on behalf of the Roman Church from Latin America to East Asia. It was succeeded in the mid-17th century by Modernity II, centered first in Amsterdam but then recentered from the 18th century on in England and Scotland. It was mercantilist and bourgeois, advocating Christianity as in Modernity I, but sending Protestant rather than Catholic missionaries to the marginalized, colonized world. Major regions, but also all the major religions, were affected by this two-pronged emergence of European Modernity, none more so than Islam and the Muslim societies of Asia and Africa, or what Hodgson calls the Afro-Eurasian ecumene. See Enrique Dussel, "The Sociohistorical Meaning of Liberation Theology (Reflections about Its Origin and World Context)" in David N. Hopkins, Lois Ann Lorentzen, Eduardo Mendieta, and David Batstone, eds., *Religions/Globalizations—Theories and Cases* (Durham, NC: Duke University, 2001): 34–35.

4   Huricihan Islamoğlu, "Islamicate World Histories" in Douglas Northrup, ed., *A Companion to World History* (Oxford: Blackwell, 2012): chapter 30, 447–463, here summarized to fit my argument for Islamicate cosmopolitan as a pervasive element of world history.

5   The complete text of Islamoğlu's (2014) WOCMES paper can be found at: https://www.academia.edu/37842112/ISLAMOGLU_ Marshall_Hodgson_and_WorldHistoryas_Fulfillment_of_Individual_ Moral_Responsibility.pdf (accessed June 24, 2020).

6   Jocelyne Dakhlia, "Harems and Cathedrals: The Question of Gender and Sexuality in the Work of Marshall Hodgson" in Burke and Mankin (2018): chapter 8. Also noteworthy is that the most accessible summary digest of *The Venture of Islam* was provided by Hodgson's last PhD student, herself a brilliant female comparativist. See "The Islamic World," an epitome by Marilyn Waldman, along with Malika Zeghal, in *Encyclopaedia Britannica* online (accessed on May 30, 2020).

2

Eastward Into India

Let me begin this chapter with a query that many of you may have been asking by now. It is perhaps the same query that has often been asked of me whenever I address the topic of Islam, and link it to civilization or cosmopolitanism. Must not Islamicate civilization always be mimetic? And must not Islamicate cosmopolitans always be nostalgic? The common assumption is that there is one singular and dominant civilization. We now call it Western or Euro-American civilization. Going back to Greek/Roman antecedents, Western civilization is the model for all civilizations; China, India, and Islam are mere copy cats of its strongest features even while providing their own regional accents. The parallel critique is made of Islamicate cosmopolitans, even when they are called Muslim or Islamic cosmopolitans, as some still prefer to do. The indebtedness is presumed to be similar to the civilization label: to be cosmopolitan is to be European or American, if not by birth at least in taste, travel, lifestyle preference. For Eurocentric triumphalists as also for their American counterparts, it is the modern West that has created what is known as cosmopolitan thought, its ideal and practice, its vision as also its limits. All other brands are either branches or copies of the original.

But fuzzy or *barzakh* logic throws up another model. It presupposes, as do those who believe in a single interdependent vision of world history, that all branches of humankind share common features,

Islamicate Cosmopolitan Spirit, First Edition. Bruce B. Lawrence.
© 2021 Bruce B. Lawrence. Published 2021 by John Wiley & Sons, Ltd.

among them privileging elites and modeling behavior on some of their best traits. In this chapter I look at two male elites, from the 11th and another from the 20th century. Their lives span the history of Islam in South Asia but also display how the Islamicate spirit enlivens the trajectory of belonging (to an empire or nation) and longing (for the betterment of humankind).

No elite scholar carries the mantle of epic human achievement, within an Islamic environment as a Muslim exemplar, more readily than does Abu Rayhan Muhammad ibn Ahmad al-Biruni, the initial subject of this chapter.

Neither Arab nor Persian but Turkish in ancestry, Biruni lived in the late 9th, early 10th century in what is now Pakistan bordering northern India. A scholar trained in multiple disciplines, Biruni benefited from royal patronage to pursue his research and writing. He was a contemporary of the well-known Ibn Sina or Avicenna, with whom he corresponded about the nature and goals of scientific research. But unlike Avicenna, Biruni synthesized a wide swath of disciplines with an accent on observation and experimentation in all that he undertook to study, describe, and publish. He is said to have written nearly 150 books. They range from astrology and astronomy to biology, geology, paleontology, optics, cartography, geodesy, mineralogy, psychology, linguistics, and mathematics. He further engaged history, religion, and philosophy, with remarkable command of languages.[1]

In other words, both culturally and linguistically Biruni was an exemplar of in-between-ness or *barzakh* logic. He was an interstitial Muslim subject, with credentials to become an exemplar of Islamicate Cosmopolitan Spirit (ICS). Though his first language was a Central Asian precursor of Uzbek, he also wrote in both Persian and Arabic, and translated from Greek, Sanskrit, and Syriac into Arabic. And so through his scientific production, Biruni secured for himself a prominent place in the pantheon of those who produced Islamicate civilization as distinctive within, but also contributing, to the Afro-Eurasian ecumene.

It is in his contribution to "the discovery of India," however, that Biruni becomes the embodiment of ICS. Other Muslims had

9

preceded him to India. Since the late 7th century there had been a thriving community of settlers, traders, and soldiers in Sind,[2] for instance, but no one before Biruni was intent to understand the cultural depth, as also the scientific advances, of Hindustan.

It can even be argued that Biruni was the pioneer of comparative studies in religion. His approach to the study of religious traditions presupposes, first of all, a genuine willingness to see truth and value in other cultures, without being forced to insist that there are universal truths in all religious traditions or, like a radical pluralist, that all cultures are equally valid in their religious and social expressions. Rather, what Biruni seems to be arguing is that there is a common human element in every culture that makes all cultures distant relatives, however foreign they might seem to one another. This is the main premise underlying his whole project. Neither a textual inference nor a mystical insight, it is one based on observation and empirical data collection (*burhan*). This theme is discernible in the passages from *India* where Biruni compares and contrasts the views and customs of different cultures.

In order to demonstrate that there is a common human element that makes all cultures distant relatives, and India central to their connection over time, Biruni starts with a critique of the available Muslim literature on Hindu culture. According to Biruni, not only was the available literature on Hinduism insufficient, it was also misleading. "Everything which exists on this subject in our literature," he complains, "is second hand information which one copied from the other, a farrago of materials never sifted by the sieve of critical examination."[3] This, according to Biruni, was inconsistent with the ethical framework provided by the Scriptures of both Christianity and Islam. He illustrates his argument by referring to the Qur'an and the Bible, respectively. The Qur'an reads, "Speak the truth, even if it were against yourselves" (Qur'an: 4, 133b); in a similar vein it is stated in the Bible that "Do not mind the fury of kings in speaking the truth before them. They only possess your body, but they have no power over your soul" (*Cf.* Matt.x.18, 19,

28; Luke xii. 4).[4] In short, it was religious and ethical concerns, more than anything else, that led Biruni to study other cultures from a comparative perspective.

And what makes him notable as an ICS paragon is his self-conscious advance of a method for comparative inquiry and analysis that he knows to be provisional yet still pivotal. He is an exponent of *barzakh* logic a millennium before its companion category, fuzzy logic, was invented in mid-20th-century America. Biruni was actually a natural philosopher, though in today's parlance he would be listed as a research scientist.[5] He was also an independent thinker, a self-conscious and self-critical comparativist.

For Biruni, comparison provided a distinctive heuristic purpose: to eradicate common misconceptions, in this case, misconceptions about Hinduism among Muslims, and in its place to promote a better acquaintanceship between two religious traditions, Islam and Hinduism. Yet Biruni was not proposing a sort of perennial philosophical view that presupposes the transcendental unity of all religions. Rather, as a believing Muslim, he simply welcomed certain differences among different peoples. In other words, he believed, as he himself stated, that "God has created the world as containing many differences in itself,"[6] and these differences should be welcomed. In order to prove his argument, he attempted to explore some of the most disputed issues, such as God, polytheism, creation, and hierarchy or the caste system in different cultures. Though he differs in many respects from Riverbend, he would applaud her axiom, earlier cited, to wit: "I wish people could be sufficiently rooted in their multiple legacies that they can allow others the sanctity of theirs."

What justifies Biruni's stature as an inclusivist who is also an exemplar of the ICS is his theological in-between-ness. Biruni treats the concept of God as a shared resource for all cultures. Even when he critiques idol worshiping in the Indian context, he limits that critique to the reflexes and practices of the uneducated class. At the same that he finds them abominable, he does not claim that they are unique to the Indian religion. What Biruni emphasizes, however, is that similar practices can be observed in even higher cultures where the division between educated and uneducated class is also evident.

Above all, Biruni could not and did not tolerate those who rejected something—whether an idea or an experiment—out of hand before seeing whether it could be useful. In other words, he was aware that anticosmopolitan thinking abounds, and he did not hesitate to criticize its exponents. His intolerance of the fool or bigot is illustrated in the following anecdote. "Once, when he showed an instrument for setting the times of prayer to a certain jurist, the latter objected that it had engraved upon it the names of the Byzantine months; this constituted an imitation of the infidels. 'The Byzantines also eat food', retorted Biruni, 'so do not imitate them in this'. After that he refrained from further discussion with this man."[7]

In his study of other religions, as in his approach to the galaxy of planets, Biruni argues that understanding is not only possible but also necessary. In both religion and science, one must begin with a phenomenological approach, looking at things as they are, and then dialogue with others in pursuit of a comparative analysis that unfolds the wonders of creation, whether in the circuit of the sky or the ambit of society. Biruni remains an Islamicate cosmopolitan because recent scholarship on him is still discovering new ways of framing his legacy. Among them is the magnificent biography by a fellow historian of science. George Malagaris summarizes Biruni's disposition as, above all, shaped by a distinctly Islamicate cosmopolitanism:

> His approach typically involved a comparative awareness of the history of a question, an investigation by means of empiricism and calculation, and frequent handling of disputation and debate. The medieval Islamic world had gone well past mere transmission of the world of late antique Hellenism. It included learning from the Franks and Chinese, as well as Jews, Zoroastrians, and the peoples of India. Al-Biruni's individual genius was expressed within that cosmopolitan context. Among his other qualities, al-Biruni was a superb synthesizer.[8]

M. F. Husain

While there are many successors to Biruni, as synthesizer, cross-cultural student, and exponent of fuzzy logic, on a millennial trajectory one looms large: M. F. Husain. Let me introduce the fuzzy, or better the *barzakh*, logic of M. F. Husain. In September 2010, Maqbool Fida Husain celebrated his 95th birthday by painting. He painted almost every day, from 4:00 to 9:00 a.m., and had painted since he was 14. Constantly traveling and moving his home base, as though to deny the logic of both boundaries and identity, he still produced over 30,000 works of art during his lifetime. Born in rural India in 1915, by the time he died in a London hospital on June 8, 2011, M. F. Husain had lived in many parts of India, Europe, and the United States, and had traveled extensively in South America and Southeast Asia. He migrated first from the Indian countryside to Bombay (now Mumbai), where he made a modest living painting street canvases. (He wore no shoes then. Actually, he never did wear shoes, though in recent years he had begun to color his toenails, and his fingernails as well.) Husain's bare feet, in the words of a defender, "always symbolized his connection to the people of India and kept him grounded in its ethos even as he rose from very humble origins to hobnob with the rich and powerful."[9] In the mid-1990s, he came to be defined as a Muslim enemy by right-wing Hindu politicians—and, in 2006, after failing to soothe his critics or find space to paint in his vast homeland, he moved first to Dubai, and then to Doha, on the invitation of Sheikha Mozhan, a member of the Qatari royal family who also became his patron.

Husain's nonagenarian years assumed an annual pattern of movement. Every spring he traveled to London, where he had a studio, then to Rome, where he had another studio, for part of the summer, then to the United States, where he had no studio but did have an ongoing project. He divided the autumn months between Dubai and Doha. But he continued to paint Indian subjects. He was Muslim but more than Muslim. He was Indian but of remote Arab lineage: his ancestors had emigrated from Yemen to Gujarat centuries

before. Born Muslim, he did not migrate to Pakistan after Parti-
tion. He identified with his country of birth in its evolution from a
British colony to the world's largest democracy. Husain embodied
the fluid-boundary logic, a variant of the *barzakh* logic that marked
the ICS, a new cosmopolitanism developing as the globe began to
shrink, through new communications technology, and also expand,
through opportunities to connect multiple sites. Husain combined
many, apparently immiscible elements that he also modified so that
all could be embraced in a seamless flow: "Nothing in creation is
useless," he once observed. "It is our duty to see how best to use it."

Nowhere was Husain more representative of a postcolonial cosmopolitan viewpoint than in his constant struggle to relate religion
to nation, and nation and to civilization. Beginning especially in the
1990s, he was held increasingly accountable to judgments about
whether he should be considered religious or secular. Some said he
was a "last gasp secularist"—one whose secularism privileged faith
and religious practice yet emphasized syncretism. It might seem that
he affirmed as much in a 2009 interview, in which he observed: "My
disposition now is not dogmatic at all. I am not a fundamentalist.
There are different faiths. The personal faith is within you, but you
have to respect everyone's faith. You're not a preacher, or reformer,
or a teacher, or a thinker. As a painter you just work with the visual,
which becomes universal. Islam is universal."[10] Others held instead
that Husain's approach to religion was secularism Indian-style:
"Indian-style secularism," Ashis Nandy wrote in 1990, "must have
space for a continuous dialogue among religious traditions but also
between the religious and the secular so that in the ultimate analysis
each of the major faiths (at least for Indians) includes within it an
in-house version of the other faiths both as internal criticisms and as
a reminder of the diversity of themes of transcendence."[11]

This kind of intercreedal, transcultural hybridity or heterology, a
form of *barzakh* logic, was not unique to Husain but it meant, at the
least, that he could not be labeled a secular agnostic or atheist in the
mold of Christopher Hitchens or Stephen Hawking. Husain's variety of secularism was intercreedal rather than noncreedal. He drew

on resources—of memory, imagination, and creativity—that deny creedal finality even while acknowledging the appeal of revealed truth and institutional patterns of liturgical observance.

How Husain regarded fluid boundaries and unresolved contradictions—both marks of the *barzakh* logic at the core of ICS—is clearest in two of his larger projects, one of which had the Mahabharata as its subject. More than 300 of Husain's works were donated by the American collectors Chester and Davida Herwitz to the Peabody Essex Museum in Massachusetts, and those that focus on the Indian epic—paintings that had been in part inspired and funded by the Herwitzes—were featured in a one-man show at the Peabody Essex Museum from late 2006 to early 2007. Underlying the exhibit was one central question: does the Mahabharata belong only to Hindus, as Husain's adversaries were asserting, or is it part of the legacy of all Indians and, furthermore, of all human beings? Husain spoke of the Mahabharata as at once bounded and boundless, national and transnational. "In his Mahabharata paintings," an Indian reviewer observed, "Husain was reaffirming that the epic had more to do with an Indian sensibility than with Hindu atavism. He is simultaneously honoring and appropriating the epic, and in offering his vision of the Mahabharata to India and the world, Husain has paid a fundamental tribute to his own civilization, one which he has, through his reinvention of the past and his re-imagining of the present, immeasurably enriched."[12]

The same could, and should, be said about Husain's approach to a second major project, which centered on Islamic Arab civilization and which he was commissioned to paint in Doha. Some questioned the depth of his new Arab patrons' commitment to Husain as a vehicle of specifically Indian values, norms, culture, and history. "The younger sheikhs and sheikhas of the Emirates have limitless largesse," Geeta Kapur noted. "They are cosmopolitan and 'progressive.' But of course they remain innocent of the complexities of the man and the artist they patronize: this post-colonial modern artist of a democratic nation to which he gave, in the moment of its birth, a pictorial language adequate to its ideal of a secular republic—and a vision that both succeeded, and failed."[13] Yet the secret of Husain's own success as an artist was his devotion to just that vision. "I have worked very hard," he said in 2010, "and I am still on my toes. I have all this energy. For the first 20 years, after I moved from a small town to Mumbai, when I was sleeping on footpaths, I never regretted what I was doing. My concentration and focus never failed. That is the test."[14]

Husain made this remark in response to a question that I asked Deena Chalabi to pose to him in 2010, when I had the opportunity to celebrate his 95th birthday at the Museum of Islamic Art in Doha. I had convened a seminar of leading scholars on modern Indian art, and we titled the event "The World Is His Canvas." But which world was Husain's canvas? By this question, I do not simply mean to ask whether his world was India, or Doha and Islam, or Europe. I mean also to ask if his canvas was the world as we observe, measure, and try to understand it—or whether the world he painted is somewhere on the edges of what is known or knowable, visible, or hidden. Husain himself answered that question during the Doha interview in 2010: "They say that for perfect art, you have to be telling a lie. What you see is an illusion. Reality is beyond that."

Husain was claiming that as an artist, he, like other artists, had to see a reality existing beyond the illusions of the sensible world, a creation of *barzakh* logic juxtaposing the knowable and unknowable, the visible and invisible. The announced theme of Husain's Doha project on Arab civilization was the relationship of Islam and Christianity. The paintings were first displayed at the opening of the Museum of Islamic Art (designed by I. M. Pei) in November 2008. Although projected to become 99 canvases, only 32 had been completed by the time of Husain's death. Some of the paintings are so small they may seem inconsequential: three men conversing, a fisherman and a falcon, a red camel against a black sky, a tea stall. Others seem didactic: to highlight the achievements of Arab science, there is a tableau tribute to Jabir ibn Hayyan and the Ikhwan as-Safa, as also to Arab astronomy. Still others evoke Husain's own ancestral country, Yemen (to which he is linked spiritually through the Suleimani subsect of the Bohras), along with a tribute to the Queen of Sheba and to a modern street scene in Sanaa. There are but three paintings in the sequence that seem to fit the ostensible theme, and what these three have in common is their effort to show how opposites elide rather than collide. These paintings do so not through attention to religious doctrine but, instead, to elements of everyday existence that Islam and Christendom share.

It has often been said that to look only at religion is to miss the point of Islam. To see only Islam is to ignore the traces of an Arab civilization that includes religion but also exceeds it. The paintings that represent Islam in Husain's series always frame religious themes or actors in contexts that divert the viewer from a creedal or even a theistic message. They capture the eclectic, resilient, inclusive spirit of Islamicate civilization—a culture not for Arabs alone, or even only for Muslims. It is the epitome of the ICS painted across time and borders:

Here is one of the most gripping of the Doha paintings, simultaneously political and transpolitical, connecting as it does, though obliquely, Bilal and Barack Obama (Figure 2.1). Integral to Husain's imagination was bringing together past and present, conjoining incongruous moments and actors in ways that seem at once fantastic and farcical, irreverent as well as implausible, yet suffused with joy and evoking celebration.

The Bilal–Obama connection was inspired by the 2008 presidential election. Husain stayed up late to listen to the results in Doha. He was so elated that he could not sleep (at age 93), and so he devoted himself to a painting of Bilal, one of the first converts to Islam—an Ethiopian. The phrase *Allahu Akbar* looms large at the bottom, with the name BILAL written across the middle of the figure with upraised arms. One has to know the painter's story of its inspiration to conclude that Obama is projected as the modern-day equivalent of Bilal. "It took America 200 years to do what Islam did in less than 10 years," Husain quipped: "make a black man its major icon to the outside world." Bilal was, of course, not Muhammad; he was only the leader of ritual prayer, not of the entire Muslim community. But the comparison does reflect Husain's ability to cross religion and

Figure 2.1 Bilal, July 1, 2010.
Source: Duke University, https://humanitiesfutures.org/papers/islamicate-
cosmopolitan-past-without-future-future-still-unfolding/.

politics, enriching one by contact with the other, while also denying
either ultimate authority over the individual. He embodies, even as
he retrieves, reinvents, and redeploys, *barzakh* logic.

Perhaps the most satisfying way to explain this variety of utopian
vision, a reflex of the ICS, is to say that Husain understood art as the
common labor of humanity. At the 95th birthday celebration, he
spoke briefly but passionately about his "philosophy." The first task of
humankind, he said, is to halter thought: "In creation, Satan was the

first one to think, and he protested against God's favoring of Adam." Thinking, then, is in principle antihuman. The second task that one has is to respond to one's deepest self, to foster, and follow, one's own potential to evolve. "Out of ten," he said, "only two or three will be evolved, yet the created order depends on their evolution." Then he added: "There are nine major religions, but there is also a tenth: humanity; and it is the basis of all the others." In an earlier interview that also took place in Doha, Husain was asked, "Can an artist or his work belong to just one country, since his work relates to so many people around the world?" To which Husain replied:

> Why artists? Any human being belongs to the world; he is a creation of God. Any human being who has evolved, not necessarily a painter or a writer, belongs to the world. He is an artist of life. Just as a writer uses words to express himself, or an artist uses images, so the ordinary human being uses life force to create a life useful to other human beings. This is also creation. Every human being belongs to the world. All distinctions are political, artificial.[15]

Barzakh logic has never had a better advocate, nor the ICS a more apt exemplar, at once grounded and unbounded, than M. F. Husain.

Notes

1   There is a large library of secondary works on Al-Biruni, and among those that deal with his contribution to what became the science of comparative religion, see the expansive summation in Kamar Oniah Kamaruzaman, *Early Muslim Scholarship in Religionswissenschaft: The Works and Contributions of Abu-Rayhan Muhammad ibn Ahmad al-Biruni* (Kuala Lumpur: International Islamic University, 2003). For Indology specifically, one must also now consult two recent publications that highlight Biruni's work with Indian/Sanskrit sources: Mario Kozah, *The Birth of Indology as an Islamic Science. Al-Bīrūnī's Treatise on Yoga Psychology* (Leiden, the Netherlands: Brill, 2015), and Mario Kozah, ed. & tr., *The Yoga Sutras of Patanjali by Abu Rayhan al-Biruni* (New York, NY: NYU Press, 2020).

2 The best study of Arab Sind remains Derryl N. MacLean, *Religion and Society in Arab Sind* (Leiden, the Netherlands: Brill, 1989).

3 Ainslee Embree, ed., *Albiruni's India* (New York, NY: W.W. Norton, 1971): 6.

4 Embree (1971): 4.

5 I am indebted to an outside reviewer who pointed out that "research science" as understood today is a modern line of inquiry, so while Biruni, like Ibn Khaldun later, performed scientific experiments and advocated scientific knowledge, neither was strictly speaking a "scientist," a term first invented by William Whelwell (in 1833), which eventually replaced "natural philosopher" during the 19th century, a period of accelerated change when "scientific revolution" forged ahead in global history.

6 Embree (1971): 24.

7 Cited from E.S. Kennedy, "Al-Biruni (or Beruni), Abu Rayhan (or Abu'l Rayhan) Muhammad Ibn Ahmad" in *Dictionary of Scientific Biography*, vol. 2 (New York, NY: Charles Scribner's Sons, 1989): 155.

8 George Malagaris, *Biruni* (Oxford: Oxford University Press, 2019; overview). Among the other elements of Biruni, unexplored in prior contributions, are two interventions at a 2016 London conference that highlighted Biruni as attracted to Shi'i perspectives and Chinese art. "C. Hillenbrand reviewed 'Biruni on Islamic history' through close reading of the sources and exposed a Shi'i element in his writing, which sits oddly with his later Ghaznavid affiliation and writings, while R. Hillenbrand analyzed the 'The miniatures in the Edinburgh manuscript of Biruni's *Chronology*' and described vividly the aesthetics and meaning of this object, along with its peculiar *chinoiserie*".

9 The quotation is from Ram Rahman, e-mail communication, June 10, 2011. Much of what follows is excerpted from Bruce B. Lawrence, "'All Distinctions are Political, Artificial': The Fuzzy Logic of M.F. Husain," *Common Knowledge* 19(2) (2013), 269–274. But since the writing and publication of this article, I have come to understand fuzzy logic as also *barzakh* logic in another register, so I use both terms to depict the distinctive edge of M. F. Husain's creativity as an Islamicate actor in the late 20th and early 21st century.

10 From Husain's March 2009 interview with Deena Chalabi.

11   Ashis Nandy, "The Politics of Secularism and the Recovery of Religion" in Veena Das, ed., *Mirrors of Violence: Communities, Riots, and Survivors in South Asia* (New Delhi: Oxford University Press, 1990): 74.

12   Shashi Tharoor, "Epic India: Paintings by M.F. Husain" in Tharoor and Susan S. Bean, eds., *Epic India: M.F. Husain's Mahabharata Project* (Salem, MA: Peabody Essex Museum, 2006): 24.

13   Geeta Kapur, "Modernist Myths and the Exile of Maqbool Fida Husain" in Sumathi Ramaswamy, ed., *Barefoot Across the Nation: Maqbool Fida Husain and the Idea of India* (London: Routledge, 2010): 51.

14   Excerpted from the March 2009 interview with Deena Chalabi.

15   From Husain's interview with Nahla Nainar, in *Gulf Times*, June 2, 2010.

3

Westward Into Spain

It is difficult to escape the symbolic significance of certain dates. September 11, 2001, popularly known as 9/11, will forever mark American accounts of modern-day Islamic terror, though British and Spanish watchers have their own dates of stealth attack, civilian death, and protracted mourning: July 2005 (with 7/7 paralleling 9/11) for the United Kingdom and March 2004 for Spain.

Though the Spanish attackers were initially said to have been Basque separatists, they were more likely Islamic extremists from nearby Morocco. Even if there proves to be some collaboration between the two groups, what stands out in all the subsequent iteration of the Spanish case is the twisted history of Islam in Spain that goes back to two further dates: 711 and 1492.

It was in 711 that the first Muslim conqueror set foot on Spanish soil. Tariq bin Ziyad not only established a Muslim military, then political, social, and cultural, presence in what had been Visigoth Spain, he began a long process of Muslim interaction with non-Muslims—Jews as well as Christians—that continued past 1492, when all Jews were expelled, and 1502, when all Muslims were expelled, till the eviction of the last Muslims from Spain in the early 17th century. The history of Islamicate Spain spans over 900 years.

What does this have to do with Islamicate cosmopolitan? And how does it explain Islamicate Cosmopolitan Spirit (ICS)? Consider geography over time. Spain is a contested sphere of many cultural and

Islamicate Cosmopolitan Spirit, First Edition. Bruce B. Lawrence.
© 2021 Bruce B. Lawrence. Published 2021 by John Wiley & Sons, Ltd.

political influences that have yet to be adequately analyzed or fully understood. Spain, even more than other contested European sites, will yield new interpretations but special preference must be given to those empirical observers of local histories, cultures, and influences that extend over the full period from 711 to 1615. Their significance is too often distorted in a presentist gaze that looks solely, or narrowly, at national history as modern. It is evident that the experience of al-Andalus, as also the earlier experiments of Frederick II (r. 1198–1250) in Sicily, influenced Hodgson in formulating, then expanding his notion of Islamicate. He lauds Frederick II for expanding cultural synergy through inspirational leadership: "The Latin rule in Sicily was unique in the Occident for its bureaucratic solidity – required because of the high-cultural level of the local population and their intimate relations with Muslims as well as Greeks; and this in turn made possible the unique role of Frederick II as disturber and ultimately inspirer of other Latin princes." But it is al-Andalus for whom he reserves the accolade for dispersing Islamicate norms to the zenith: "It was in the Spanish peninsula where imitation and adaptation of Islamicate ways was at its height, and whence they were most regularly spread over Europe. Here perhaps more than anywhere else it was the tremendous prestige of Muslim learning that persuaded Occidentals to study works in Arabic that they did not trouble to study in the original Greek."[1]

It is difficult to overstate the emphasis that Hodgson placed on "the tremendous prestige of Muslim learning" and its impact on Occidental thinking. "The most important consequence of the translations from Arabic was to raise Occidental thinking to a higher level of sophistication." It was not any particular text or set of texts but their collective impact, "in the form of the challenge to the imagination posed by the very existence at such close range of Islamicate sophistication." More difficult to trace is the penetration of Islamicate themes and methods in the field of aesthetic culture but since "art, above all, transforms whatever it feeds upon … probably in this realm also the most important consequence of the Islamicate presence was its challenge to the imagination."[2] Yet, instead of the term "Islamicate," many art historians of al-Andalus resort to using inverted commas to describe the synergy of the art they are studying. One example is Cynthia Robinson, perhaps the foremost contemporary scholar of Alhambra, the icon of Andalusian architecture, linked to the Nasrid dynasty, itself the last Islamic dynasty to survive in premodern Spain. (It was the Nasrid defeat that led to the expulsion of the Moors in 1502 under the newly united Catholic kingdoms of Castile and Aragon.) Robinson avoids use of "Islamicate" and instead asks the question: how "Oriental" is the Alhambra? Whenever she is confronted by an unclear association in a key term, she places that term in inverted commas. Hence she explores how certain elements were either "Gothic" or "Islamic" or both but resists describing later Andalusian ornamental culture, that is, *mudejar* art, as "Islamic art appropriated by Christians or Jews." Moving beyond any ascriptive vocabulary, she instead opts to define *mudejar* ornamental vocabulary through a series of abstract qualities: "as the product of an ongoing process of iteration and reiteration receiving important input from all participant parties, resulting in a visual language which, despite being an aniconic one, was used in the articulation of a wide range of aesthetic, devotional, and polemical content."[3]

On the other hand, one does find Islamicate used, albeit ambiguously, by a prominent historian of premodern Spanish history. Brian Catlos introduces the term Islamicate to distinguish the post-Nasirid period, when after the 1492 Reconquista and the 1502 expulsion, some Muslim residents of Spain elected to stay rather than leave al-Andalus. In *Muslims of Medieval Latin Christendom, c. 1050–1640*, he observes that "those Muslims secretly practicing Islam, these so-called 'Moriscos', were finally forcibly expelled from the kingdoms of Spain in the years between 1609 and 1615. This marked the conclusion of nine hundred years of Islam in Iberia, the extinction, after five centuries, of the last Muslim communities of what had been the world of Latin

Christendom." And then in a footnote he explains the problem
with using the term "Moriscos":

*Morisco, from "moro" ("Muslim"), means "Islamicate," rather than
"Moorish."* "Moor" has been generally abandoned as a term for
referring to Muslims of Christian Spain. It conveys a racial/ethnic
dimension (in reference to "Mauritania" or Morocco, or the early
modern English "Blackamoor") that supports the distorting and
inaccurate idea that these people were of North African origin.
Few were; in the late Middle Ages, the great majority of Muslims in
the peninsula were the descendants of indigenous converts, or had
ancestors who had been living there for centuries.[4]

The footnote changes the tone of all that precedes and follows it. The substitution of "Islamicate" for "Morisco," while a
brilliant, productive use of Hodgson's neologism, could only apply
as a qualifier not as a substitute category. In other words, there
could be Islamicate Jews or Christians but not Islamicates, especially since the Islamicate qualifier has greater applicability than
to the last phase of Hispanic Muslim minority existence after the
forced conversions of the 16th century. But as a qualifier Islamicate
does ferret out more than clandestine subterfuges in a hegemonic
Iberian Catholic realm. It also reclaims the pervasive influence of
Muslim practices apart from the confessional boundaries of Islam
and Christianity. It could also apply to revaluing the Muslim experience, at once protracted and fluid, in neighboring Sicily as well as
al-Andalus. Looking at the period of Roger II (r. 1130–1154), who
preceded Frederick II, discussed above, we find a Christian ruler
who made use not only of Muslim subjects but Muslim aesthetic
tastes and culinary practices. In examining the Roger II's rule, Catlos notes how local circumstances often dictated the ebb and flow
of religious allegiances. Indeed, Catlos' methodical inquiry crisscrosses the Mediterranean and veers into eastern Europe: he compares the varied experiences of Muslims from Iberia to southern
Italy up to Hungary. There was more diversity than conformity,
with ideological currents shaping and reshaping what it meant to

be Islamicate subjects, subjects at once linked to Islam historically and culturally yet with variant experiences, memories, and projections of themselves as Muslim and European.

Islamicate, or better ICS, is, can, and should be expanded in both its temporal and spatial scope. It is more than Muslim. As we noted at the outset, Islamicate extends beyond Muslim self-identity. It refers to the social and cultural dimensions of Muslim rule that are informed by Islamic belief but not limited to Muslims. ICS is about a style of life, a sense of beauty, and a mode of conduct as much as it is about a creedal or liturgical performance. Christians could also be Islamicate. Elsewhere Catlos asserts: "The outward distinctiveness of Christians and Muslims was further undermined by the profound engagement of the Christians of Iberia with Islamicate culture, in terms of dress, language, and quotidian culture."[5] Of course, there was competition and even enmity at some levels, yet the everyday or quotidian culture projected norms that crossed ethnic, religious, and social boundaries. The ground-level history of post-1500 Spain reveals the engagement of non-Muslims in Islamicate cosmopolitan practices and preferences, norms and values, across greater Iberia.

Catlos' insight into translation sharpens the focus on why Islamicate cosmopolitan can, and should, be used to describe activities in al-Andalus even before the Reconquista of 1492. Crucial was the high period of intellectual exchange 1100–1450 CE and its exceptional engagement in translation activity.

> This scientific enterprise [of translation from Arabic to Latin] was carried out to a great extent by the same clergy who were involved in developing anti-Muslim polemic. Robert of Ketton, the Qur'an translator, had been drawn to Arabic and the Islamic world out of his interest in astrology, and after completing his commission for Peter the Venerable, served as Archdeacon of Pamplona. Arnau de Vilanova, who translated a series of medical treatises in Montpellier in the late 1200s was a fervent anti-Muslim. But science comprised a sort of intellectual 'neutral zone', all but devoid of polemic, in which intellectuals of different faiths could collaborate without evoking their ideological personae. And whereas, previously, the translation

effort was imagined as being carried out by Christians with the collaboration of *Islamicate Jews*, it is clear that subject Muslims were also engaged in this process, and to a far greater degree than is acknowledged in the texts themselves. This was the case not only in Palermo, where the Norman court carried out an explicit program of patronage of Arabic arts and letters practiced by Muslims, but across the Latin Mediterranean, where both free scholars and slaves either collaborated willingly or were pressed into service. Here, translation was sponsored not only by Arabophiles such as Roger II and Frederick II, but even by less personally sympathetic figures, like Charles II. In the Iberian kingdoms many Muslims served as official, royal translators of Arabic (as did Jews), and in the sixteenth century the program to catalog and translate the Arabic holdings of the imperial library was entrusted to Moriscos.[6]

Catlos's observations are expansive but not conclusive. I am left wondering how the internal register of self—what Catlos later catalogues as moral, institutional, and affective tangents—operated among those engaged in these labors. I wince when "Islamicate" is used, as it is here, only to depict Jews (*Islamicate Jews*) but not otherwise applied to Iberian actors across Islamdom, laboring at the doorstep of nascent Europe. Why is it not also used instead of "Morisco," to refer to Muslim and non-Muslim subjects of al-Andalus, especially since Catlos earlier had underscored the unacceptability of Morisco as a racialized term, one that could/should be replaced by Islamicate?

Beyond these disjunctures, and the corrections they require, I am grateful for the critical historical revisionism at work in Catlos's study. It highlights a double affirmation: (a) despite competing test cases from Italy (both Sicily[7] and Venice),[8] Iberia remains a crucial locus for any exploration of how Islamicate cosmopolitan exists, at once pervading and transforming bounded religious identities; and also, (b) at the core of the Islamicate Iberian cosmopolitan self is an unfulfilled sense of connection, an emergent sensibility of spirit, expanding the Islamicate self to a universal ethos of beauty and justice, at once challenging and changing the imagination of non-Muslims and Muslims alike.

It is on this second point that Catlos takes a stride that few have ventured before him. He views Muslim Spain not through a single but a triple lens. Almost as an addendum to Part Two of his magisterial work, he raises the most difficult question: what does it all mean? He prefaces his own answer with an awareness of the time in which he writes, with its dark background noises about Islam and Muslims.

> The distance of time may make some uncomfortable subjects easier to address, but that is evidently not the case with Muslim–Christian relations in the Middle Ages. The events of 9/11, the long history of Western colonization and subjugation of North Africa and the Muslim Near East, Zionism and the Palestinian "problem," the war in Iraq (and the apparently impending war in Iran), "jihadism," al-Qaeda, programs of Christian mission and Western "modernization," academic and popular "Orientalism," notions of papal infallibility, and of European superiority, not to mention plain old nativism, self-righteous religious prejudice, racism, and chauvinism, or the often equally visceral reactions against all of these, whether nostalgic or deliberately corrective – all make it difficult even for scholars to take a detached view of the history of the era of the Christian–Muslim conflict and Latin irredentism.[9]

Despite this noise, and in the face of resistance/rejection in many quarters, Catlos tries to conjure an accurate, if ambiguous, image in what he depicts as "a distant, broken mirror": medieval or premodern Spain. Catlos holds up a new triad, what he labels a macro, meso, and micro dimension, to make sense of the entire Mediterranean world. Each stratum has its own corresponding rhetorical register that he also explains: moral, institutional, affective tangents are analogous to Freud's super-ego, ego, and id. Yet they overlap, for while formal identity, the functional self, and libidinous or emotive appetite, the affective self, must be treated as separate modes, both are shaped and reshaped by the moral self, so much so that "any given individual participates in each of these modes of identity simultaneously, evoking each in specific circumstances."[10] The moral self is the third but also the capstone of these three elements. It warrants close scrutiny, beyond its deft introduction, then application to Muslim Spain by Catlos.

The best tool to grasp this set of combined elements is fuzzy or *barzakh* logic. Each explorer—whether an academic or a tourist or a casual reader—must use *barzakh* logic to break down dyadic views of Spain—as Muslim or Christian, Mediterranean or European, North or South, peaceful and harmonious, or violent and divided—and instead understand a spirited sensibility, one where the moral and affective elements are as central as their formal and emotive companions. And also where one can uphold the irreducible separation of borders without compromising their internal integrity. It is the spirit or moral core of Islamicate cosmopolitan, a form of *barzakh* logic, that begs to be defined. It cannot be reduced to English or a European language; it requires attention to two technical words, both Arabic: *taskhir* and *adab*. Each is valued, both are needed, to convey a sense of reciprocity (*taskhir*), crucial for all hierarchical societies, that also merges with a notion of *adab*, that is, performance on behalf of, and in search of, the greater good.

An Excursus on *Taskhir* and *Adab*

That imaginative leap, from social history to moral philosophy, can best be made through another Andalusian figure, often lost in the esoteric world of Sufi philosophy, but in fact germane to cosmopolitan thinking and to a cosmopolitan perspective not less Islamicate for being hierarchical.

It is too easy to forget about the most defining characteristic of empires: they are hierarchical; there is no claim for, or option to pursue, equality. Yet there is a pervasive morality; it is embodied in the Arabic word *taskhir*. Vincent Cornell, a leading scholar of premodern Islamic social thought, unpacks its relevance across time.

The reciprocal nature of the relationship between the sultan and his flock was acknowledged in theological and moral writings. The

Spanish Sufi Ibn al-'Arabi (d. 1240), who was born to a family of notables from Murcia and who demonstrates upper-class values in his works, saw the reciprocity that characterized relations between patrons and clients as mirroring the reciprocity that pertained between God and the world. This reciprocity, which Ibn al-'Arabi[11] termed 'mutual exploitation' (*taskhir*), meant that although a higher order of being or social status (such as God or the sultan) might exploit or subjugate the lower orders (humanity or the flock), a lower order might also "exploit" or constrain a higher order. According to Ibn al-'Arabi, higher orders subjugate lower orders through an act of will (*taskhir bi-l-irada*); this is part of the nature of things. God exploits humans so that they serve him; humans exploit animals, plants, and minerals for shelter and sustenance; animals exploit plants for sustenance; and plants exploit minerals. But the divine economy of justice also imposes a "return" on this exploitation, for if exploitation were unrequited, the moral balance of the universe would be upset. Thus the lower orders have the right to exploit or constrain the higher orders by virtue of their subservient status (*taskhir bi-l-hal*).

Cornell then goes on to consider a second kind of *taskhir*. "The second kind is the *taskhir* by the 'state' or 'situation'; like the *taskhir* exercised by the subjects over their king who is charged with the task of taking care of them, e.g., defending and protecting them, fighting the enemies who attack them, and preserving their wealth and their lives, etc. In all these things, which are the *taskhir* by the state, the subjects 'subjugate' their sovereign because the king is compelled to act in a certain way." And so, concludes Cornell, "justice in the medieval Muslim world was more about proportionality than equality. The root meaning of *'adl*, the Arabic word for justice, does not connote equality in the sense of sameness, but rather conveys the idea of equalizing, or restoring balance… Corrective justice entails restoring the fair balance that has been lost, but it does not mean achieving equality as defined and pursued in liberal philosophy, whether democratic or socialist."[12]

This accent on *taskhir* does not stand alone. It is inseparable from *adab*, which reinforces its daily practice through behaviors that are not limited to Islam but expressed through Muslim idioms in Islamicate societies and therefore must be grounded in the foundational scripture for all Muslims, the Qur'an, but not in a single language. On this point Shahab Ahmed helpfully underscores the value of Arabic and related texts—each with pre-text and con-text—defining what they are and how they apply to human conduct. *Adab* has a long pre-Islamic history; it can refer to literature, but it is elevated literature, at once linked to religion by its preferred form (poetry) but also its daily performance (along with prayer, labor, and leisure activity). "Arabic, Persian, Turkish and Urdu *adab* is neither imaginable, nor meaningful," observes Ahmed, "without the active imaginative unfolding of the Muslim engagement with the idea of Divine Revelation (exemplified in the Qur'ān) in the literary trajectories of self-exploration and self-expression."[13]

Crucial to that imaginative unfolding is what I call "performance," not just verbal but physical. It involves a common set of behavioral traits, morally underpinned by a notion of collective good. As I have noted elsewhere, "*adab* can and should be seen as a heuristic element at the center of rethinking Islamicate civilization in world history. While Islamicate civilization projects belief and ritual, doctrine and law, shaped by Islamic perspectives, it is not limited to them. It exceeds them especially in its concern for the often taken-for-granted ways that patterns of conduct emerge. Islamicate civilization is as much about implicit ethical norms [*adab*] as it is about explicit juridical codes [*shari'ah*]. It is as much about difference between regions and traditions as it is about sameness, collapsing geographical and cultural differences with an umbrella concept such as *ummah*. It is as much about discontinuity over time as it is about continuity."[14]

In elaborating the social dimensions of *adab* over time, the sociologist Armando Salvatore, cited earlier, has demonstrated how it functions to provide what he calls "flexible institutionalization." "The inner codes of interaction among Muslim elites," argues Salvatore, "rested on a time-honored, indeed pre-Islamic, high culture and continued to figure prominently in the production of patterns of civility. Their culture was mostly associated with the notion of *adab* and related practices… *Adab* should be considered as a parallel knowledge tradition that Islamicate civilization inherited from Persianate court culture… *Adab* embraces the ensemble of the ethical and practical norms of virtuous and beautiful life ideally cultivated by a class of literati… Far from being eclipsed with the collapse of the High Caliphate, which by and large represented an extension of Persianate rule, *adab* became particularly influential during the Middle Periods [with traces continuing into the modern era]."[15]

The Example of Ibn Khaldun

One of the exemplars for Islamicate cosmopolitan analysis, often mentioned by Salvatore, is Ibn Khaldun. Like Hodgson, Ibn Khaldun has been lauded chiefly for a single, monumental book. Hodgson refers to the *Muqaddimah*, as "no doubt the best general introduction to Islamicate civilization ever written." Notes another seasoned comparativist, Nile Green, "for Hodgson the *Muqaddimah* provided penetrating lenses for viewing world history that were polished long before the rise of the West."[16] So it is not just fitting but also necessary to review his larger profile as an aspirant to the ICS.

Ibn Khaldun was also linked to Andalusia prior to the Reconquista. A Maghribi juridical philosopher turned historian, Abd al-Rahman Ibn Khaldun (d. 1406) came from a family that had migrated from al-Andalus to the Maghrib. Like Biruni, he accepted the patronage system or *taskhir*, outlined above. But unlike Biruni, Ibn Khaldun strove to use his political wisdom to benefit one of the actual rulers of his day. Moving from one court to another, he became disillusioned and retired to Mamluk Cairo as a judge. His life, like al-Biruni's, demonstrated the importance and the constraints of royal patronage as a stimulant to intellectual creativity, while in the *Muqaddimah* (an introduction to his multivolume world history) he used his double training in philosophy and law to discern patterns in history. His outlook, like Biruni's, was at once pragmatic and inclusive or cosmopolitan. Applying the method of *burhan*, he believed that every observer has to refine and theorize what you observe in actual human exchange. Whereas Muslim historians conventionally subscribed to the view that God passed sovereignty and hegemony (*dawlah*) from one dynasty to another through His divine wisdom, Ibn Khaldun explained how it appeared in terms of a cycle of natural stages that followed an almost inevitable pattern. He ascribed the success of tribally organized migratory peoples to their stronger sense of consensus or group solidarity. It allowed them to acquire military superiority over settled peoples but their superiority, in turn, was diminished once the founding figures or early generations ceased to control the fissiparous instincts of their kinship group. As the family disperses itself among sedentary peoples and ceases to live the hard life of migration, it becomes soft from the prosperity it has brought and begins to degenerate. Internal rivalries, often fueled by personal jealousies, force one member of the family to become a king who must rely on mercenary troops and undermine his own prosperity by paying for them. In the end, the ruling dynasty falls prey to a new tribal group with fresh group feeling. The problem was circular: civilization could not survive without military prowess, yet military prowess in itself was unstable.

How does this make Ibn Khaldun a charter member of Islamicate cosmopolitan seekers, an embodiment of ICS? While there are others who contributed to the ICS, Ibn Khaldun stands out for his interstitial or *barzakh* logic, his rigorous pursuit of in-between-ness. Civilization at its core equals culture writ large over space and time. Space predominates. The geographical lens of premodern civilization focuses on the breadth of the Afro-Eurasian ecumene, as Hodgson and also Islamoğlu have noted. Civilization presupposes cities, commerce, travel and trade, warfare and alliances, and so by its very nature civilization in general but Islamicate civilization in particular should strive to be cosmopolitan. And while Ibn Khaldun makes the strongest case for the durably cosmopolitan nature of Islamicate civilization, he also stops short of reifying or claiming its apogee at one place at one time or with one dynasty.

33

Crucially Ibn Khaldun was a product of the 14th-century Mediterranean world. What distinguished him was neither his Arab lineage nor his linkage to Berbers via marriage but his Mediterranean location. At the intersection of Jewish, Christian, and Muslim influences, heir to Greek science and Arabic poetry, connected by trade and history to Asia, the Mediterranean Sea had become the nexus of Islamicate cosmopolitanism by the 14th century.[17] Social mobility as well as physical travel animated Mediterranean Muslims, especially those, like Ibn Khaldun, who rose to high posts in government, law, and education. But this background only identifies the opportunities that Ibn Khaldun either inherited or developed owing to his socio-economic background and the political circumstances of his era. The defining difference in his cosmopolitan outlook was his quest to find the points of convergence between seemingly distinct, and often competitive, elements common to elite urban Muslims in al-Andalus, the Maghrib, and Egypt.

Indeed, the biggest difference between Ibn Khaldun and other elites of his generation was his orientation to *adab*.[18] Though trained as a *faqih* or jurist and familiar with all the ancillary sciences of *fiqh* (jurisprudence), Ibn Khaldun was also an *adib* or litterateur. A litterateur is attentive to words, to their expression in both speech and writing but especially, to their polyvalence. Words can mean many things in different times, places, and contexts, and they have moral as well as literary valence when used by an *adib* exercising *adab*. Above all, an *adib* makes *adab* the instrument and the catalyst for *barzakh* thinking by his performance of migratory language, using the same word differently or multiple words to move beyond a limited range of meaning. Though this may seem a truism today, it was far from accepted knowledge or the dominant outlook, even among the notables whom Ibn Khaldun knew and whom he engaged in discussion or debate.

And so Ibn Khaldun is first marked as an ICS charter member by his use of the same words with different connotations, in different contexts, for different audiences in his classic work, the *Muqaddimah*. He is not ambiguous but ambivalent in his use of key terms such as *badawah* and *hadarah*. He also coins new terms such as *'umran* and *'asabiyah* with a specific range of meanings, one of which may be to amplify the notion of a known word, as *'asabiyah* deftly does with the juridical concept of consensus.

Reliance on metaphor allows Ibn Khaldun to demonstrate how the same word, like the same event or person, can be viewed differently over time, and also from different places in the same time frame. Perhaps the most crucial argument that Ibn Khaldun makes on behalf of history as an Islamic science is that historians alone among Muslim scientists can explain how Islam arose out of a context of orality and nomadism/primitivism (*badawah*) to become a proponent of both writing and civilization (*hadarah*). What had been speech and a habit became writing and a craft.[19] Yet the very lifeline of Islam depended on maintaining the connection between literacy and orality, between writing and speech, as also between civilized and nomad. In short, analogy, while it had its most immediate application in law, could, and should, also be applied to the understanding of the laws of history, above all, the history of Islamicate civilization.

And the nature of *networked* knowledge is also a second, decisive difference between Ibn Khaldun and other cosmopolitan elites of his day. In all aspects of his labor, Ibn Khaldun accepted, and often applauded, the achievements of his predecessors, the vast *network* of a knowledge class (the *'ulama*) who undergirded Muslim society, but at the same time he introduced a difference. While it seems impossible today to imagine any civilization without attention to the multiple networks that create and sustain its urban nodes, this insight was not fully appreciated in the late 14th century anywhere within the Afro-Eurasian ecumene, itself a matrix of intersecting, and often competing, networks.

In order to establish his new science, Ibn Khaldun the jurist had to both affirm his own practice of Tradition criticism (based on *bayan*)[20] while allowing for an empirical approach human social organization (based on *burhan*), the cornerstone, in his view, of a global civilization that encompassed the known world (*al-ma'mura min al-'ard*).[21] In effect, he used his talent as an *adib* to further his project as a *faqih*, invoking the law while opening it up to a new arena of thought. It was his forensic skill as a litterateur that allowed him to cite Event (*khabar*), itself an ancillary part of Tradition (*hadith*) scholarship, as an independent term conveying the surplus of meaning that he wanted to impart to the study of human social organization or the history of world civilization. Demarcating Tradition from Event, while affirming both, became the pathway to his new science.

Many have described Ibn Khaldun's new science as critical history, comparative sociology, or even supply-side economics. I think that another descriptor is necessary. It is not only fitting but also overdue to acknowledge Ibn Khaldun as an Islamicate cosmopolitan. The proof? The proof is what we have just described: his subtle, consistent use of language to further empirical observation as the cornerstone for networked knowledge, but also the long lag time between what he proposed and his broad acceptance in multiple fields of academic inquiry.

Malek Bennabi—A Marginal Nationalist, an Islamicate Cosmopolitan

While civilizational and cosmopolitan do overlap, they have different emphases. In the aftermath of what Hodgson calls the Great Western Transmutation, no Muslim scholar from the Afro-Eurasian ecumene can, or does, compete on even terms with Euro-American rivals. A major instance would be a modern North African whose life contrasts with Ibn Khaldun. Just as the latter was a forerunner of civilization belongings and cosmopolitan longings in an Islamicate register, so Malek Bennabi may be considered a precursor of Islam in the new millennium, at once an exemplar of the ICS and a test case of its limits.

Malek Bennabi (1905–1973), trained as an electrical engineer in Paris, now enjoys a rebirth in Algeria as both an Islamic loyalist and a radical modernist. Following his studies in Paris, Bennabi could not return to Algeria immediately after the 1962 revolution because of his pro-Islamic stance. He lived in Egypt for a time before returning to Algiers, where he then held weekly salons, or open meetings, in both Arabic and French until his death in 1973.

Bennabi's stance serves as a counterpoint to political Islam, with its focus on the public domain of government and governance, alliances and rivalries, interests and strategies. But at the same time, Bennabi does not advocate the slippery project known as Islamization of knowledge. Instead of making modernity Islamic, he advocates revisiting, and reinvigorating, the roots of Islamicate civilization. Bennabi focuses on the religious principle at the heart of every civilizational endeavor, but especially Islam. It is not enough to be Muslim, he argues, *one must be a reasoning, rational subject*, in short, a thinking individual who scans the repertoire of modern science and professional skill sets with unflinching honesty.

Bennabi advocates precisely the kind of moral rather than instrumental reasoning that Hannah Arendt, the German-American political theorist (d. 1975), had prized consistently from her earliest writings. What stands forth is the combination of *bayan* (text knowledge), *'irfan* (mystical insight), and *burhan* (empirical evidence) but with an accent on *burhan* as emotive and aesthetic, not just experimental and didactic.[22] To the extent that one relies on moral principles, in Bennabi's view, it is only through a ceaselessly probing endeavor to connect with first principles. It is the moral Muslim subject who embodies the distinctive aesthetic sensibility that has everywhere marked the greatness of Islamic civilization. It is neither bureaucracies nor business ventures that evoke the hope of the future for Islamic creativity. True creativity requires instead "deep knowledge of the structures of professions, of the workings of productive organizations, attention to detail and method, diligence and perseverance in application." Such dedication to the creative spirit is not incidental or additive; it is foundational and necessary. It must precede "the successful transplantation of modern economies into the post-colonial Muslim world."[23] Education at all levels is the key to this still abstract yet morally profound agenda.

In effect, Bennabi tries to be explicitly interstitial, to walk the tightrope between authenticity and modernity in two contexts. He acknowledges the superiority of European/Western culture in the public sphere but at the same time projects the resilience of Islamic norms, and the opportunity for Islamic values, to supplement, not replace, the instruments of a high-tech, postindustrial and postcolonial world.

If others are interstitial by inference, Bennabi is explicit in his embrace of seeming opposites. He refuses to be bound by place. It is neither location in the Maghrib nor in Europe that determines one's outlook but *bi-location*—the experience of two worlds, the imperial world of Europe and the colonial world of North Africa, and the awareness of both—that defines one's primary identity, orientation, and worldview. His is not a revamped Aristotelian logic or a version of Hegelian dialectic reasoning. Instead, he sees a gray world, pursuing his own version of fuzzy or better *barzakh* logic. "Post-colonialism in Algeria," notes the semiotician, Walter Mignolo, "is not the same as post-colonialism in France … Bennabi's reflections before, during, and after the eight years of the Algerian war (1954–1962) transcended the events and brought the discussion back home to Algeria, rather than letting it remain in Paris, counting in France's history."[24]

While Bennabi's views could be compared to those of Camus or Sartre, in fact, they were more similar to Fanon's albeit in a religious not a racial trajectory. Both Fanon and Bennabi experienced Europe, especially its higher education in the humanities and sciences, but remained grounded in Africa. "The meaning of the Algerian war in France," comments Mignolo, "was embedded in the history of France and European imperialism, while the meaning of the Algerian war in Algeria was imbedded in the history of North Africa and the enduring histories of colonialism."[25] And unless one accepted place as primary in fashioning one's authentic self, one could not aspire to the higher spirit, in Bennabi's case, an ICS. Bennabi was a conceptual idealist constrained by psychological realism: Algeria after independence remained a colonized country; it could not be truly free until it faced the burden of its colonial past, which included the susceptibility to be colonized. For that lingering susceptibility, Bennabi coined a new term, *colonisabilité*, the disposition to be colonized or to remain bound by colonial ways of thinking. In order to reverse the uncritical acceptance of norms, values, and concepts from the dominant French (or British or American) power, one had to revisit the colonization of knowledge. In short, one had to reconstruct a new edifice of civilization.

And for Bennabi the clarion cry for an intellectual struggle was *jihad fikri. Jihad fikri* required inaugurating fresh thinking and new beginnings. It acknowledged opposites without reducing their force, engaging them reciprocally in a perpetual dance of *barzakh* logic. Though it has gone unanswered in post-1991 Algeria, *jihad fikri* insists on thought, and the need to think beyond a postcolonial epistemic framework within the Muslim world. His is a visionary project rather than a pragmatic program. It does not have a stream of followers, either in North Africa or beyond, but those who deem rooted cosmopolitanism to be the strongest marginal ethos of the 21st century can, and should, see Malek Bennabi as a worthy successor to Ibn Khaldun, like him joined in the galaxy of exemplars for the undying ICS.

Notes

1   Marshall G.S. Hodgson, *The Venture of Islam: Conscience and History in a World Civilization*, Vol. II (Chicago, IL: University of Chicago Press, 1974): 364–365. There are a few popular histories that have followed Hodgson's lead in looking at the breadth of Islamicate learning, across the Maghrib into al-Andalus. One exception is Firas Alkhateeb, *Lost Islamic History: Reclaiming Muslim Civilization from the Past* (London: Hurst & Company, 2014). An entire chapter (chapter 7) is devoted to al-Andalus, yet its broad-brush treatment of premodern Spanish history does not highlight the institutional hierarchies, discursive

traditions, and performative processes found in Brian Catlos; see his 2014 monography examined in detail below.

2 Alkhateeb (2014): 366–367.

3 Cynthia Robinson, "Locating the Alhambra: A Fourteenth-Century 'Islamic' Palace and its 'Western' Context" in Finbarr Barry Flood and Gülru Necipoğlu, eds., *A Companion to Islamic Art and Architecture*, Vol. II (Oxford: Wiley-Blackwell, 2017): 726. The problem with comparing/contrasting "Islamic" with "Western" art is addressed in the conclusion.

4 Brian Catlos, *Muslims of Medieval Latin Christendom, c. 1050–1640* (Cambridge University Press, 2014): 16. To reclaim Morisco, one can look at literary culture, as Barbara Fuchs does in her monograph, *Exotic National: Maurophilia and the Construction of Early Modern Spain* (Philadelphia, PA: University of Pennsylvania Press, 2008), focusing on the lay genres of Maurophilia—the ballad, chivalric romance, historical novel—to prize "Moorishness as distinct from Islam and its attendant practices" (p. 6). A parallel effort to escape the negative implications of "Moor," in this case by looking at material culture, is Olivia Remie Constable, *To Live Like a Moor: Christian Perceptions of Muslim Identity in Medieval and Early Modern Spain* (Philadelphia, PA: University of Pennsylvania Press, 2018). Especially the nimble introduction explores how different generations of Muslim converts to Christianity retained their "Islamic" preferences—in clothes, food, and conduct—despite their changed religious identity. "Granadan cultural practices, such as styles of dress, haircuts, use of henna, and visits to bath-houses," persisted till the late 16th century. Would they not be better framed as "Islamicate Christians" instead of the derisive Morisco? (I am indebted to Michele Lamprakos for her forensic attention to the issue of Morisco/Islamicate nomenclature, and for introducing me to Fuchs as a source for further inquiry. She is not responsible for my arguments or conclusions).

5 Catlos (2014): 472. This reflects the same observation made by both Fuchs and Constable, but with reference to Islamicate as the decisive qualifier of material culture and everyday life.

6 Catlos (2014): 347–348.

7 Sicily experienced almost two centuries of Arab rule (902–1071) followed by another two centuries of generous Norman patronage

(1071–1282), auguring the Italian renaissance. Much could be said about the 12th-century Cappella Palatina in Palermo as a precursor and parallel to the kind of ICS evident in southern Spain, as an outside reviewer helpfully reminded me. While Muslim-Christian Sicily has been widely explored, notably in Alex Metcalfe, *Muslims of Medieval Italy* (Edinburgh: Edinburgh University Press, 2009) and Joshua C. Birk, *Norman Kings of Sicily and the Rise of Anti-Islamic Critique: Baptized Sultans* (London: Palgrave-Macmillan, 2016), neither author ventures to use new key words, such as Islamicate or Latinate, as does Catlos (Catlos does cite Metcalfe as one of his sources, even as he makes the case for a polysemous Islamicate culture in Sicily as also southern Spain; Catlos (2014): 472, n. 24).

8   On the centrality and ambiguity of Venice as a test case for Islamic-Christian mutual acceptance despite military rivalry, see Francesa Trivellato, "Renaissance Italy and the Muslim Mediterranean in Recent Historical Work," *The Journal of Modern History* 82(March) (2010), 127–155. "Nowhere has a positive appreciation of the aesthetic borrowings from the East been more pronounced than in a successful exhibition, Venice and the Islamic World, 828–1797, that opened at the Metropolitan Museum in March 2007. Its principal curator defines Venice's relations with the Islamic Near East as guided by an 'almost perfect balance and interaction of religious spirit, chameleonic diplomacy, and an unsentimentally practical mercantile system.' In Venice, miniatures, tapestries, brocades, porcelains, book covers, metalwork, and other luxury objects went on display in the large room of the Palazzo Ducale in which the rulers of the Venetian republic assembled until 1797. The opening panel and the affordable, abridged guide posited that 'Venice was always to maintain a rational approach to the Islamic world.' Yet those visitors who happened to raise their eyes above the glass cases containing magnificent artifacts saw massive paintings representing the Venetian participation in the Fourth Crusade, two naval battles against the Turks fought in the 1470s, and celebrations of the Venetian military commander at Lepanto (1571). The adjacent rooms host even more belligerent anti-Ottoman representations. True, many of these paintings date to after 1577, when a fire destroyed much of the Ducal Palace and a

more aggressive anti-Ottoman discourse emerged in Venice after the battle of Lepanto. *The disjuncture between the exhibition's message and its setting was nonetheless startling.*" (p. 152) I italicize the final summary statement because it embodies the difficulty of a binary logic that has to either salute tolerance (religious) or underscore violence (political). Both coexist in the alternative sphere of *barzakh* logic; it is not one or the other but their coexistence, and persistence, that must always engage the pragmatic observer.

9   Catlos (2014): 517.

10 Catlos (2014): 527. The performative nature of Islamicate habits and customs, from visual structures to dietary practices, is difficult to overstate but also elusive to trace. I have not perused the growing literature on this topic in Spanish, but an outside reviewer did guide me to one resource in English by an expert in Iberian literature: Vincent Barletta, *Covert Gestures: Crypto-Islamic Literature as Cultural Practice in Early Modern Spain* (Minneapolis, MN: University of Minnesota Press, 2005).

11 Considered one of the foremost Sufi philosophers from the premodern Islamicate world, Muhammad Muhyiddin Ibn 'Arabi was born in Seville in 1165 and died in Damascus in 1240. He traveled and wrote extensively, with more than 300 works to his credit. For his approach to the Divine Names, of which he was a visionary interpreter, see Bruce Lawrence, *The Qur'an: A Biography* (New York, NY: Atlantic Monthly Press, 2006): 108–118.

12 Vincent J. Cornell, "Ibn Battuta's Opportunism: The Networks and Loyalties of a Medieval Muslim Scholar" in miriam cooke and Bruce B. Lawrence, eds., *Muslim Networks from Hajj to Hip-Hop* (Chapel Hill, NC: University of North Carolina, 2005): 35–36. The case of Ibn Battuta, like that of the late 19th-century British adventurer, Richard Burton, illustrates the fallacy of linking cosmopolitanism to travel, multilingualism, and immersion in numerous, disparate cultures. In K. Anthony Appiah, *Cosmopolitanism: Ethics in the World of Strangers* (New York, NY: Norton/Penguin, 2006), both Ibn Battuta and Burton are lauded in what amounts to a Hellenic, European claim to cosmopolitanism as the high side of moral relativism. I argue here that Islamicate cosmopolitan must be grounded

in moral sensibilities that combine social reciprocity with attention to the larger good, a non–Hellenic claim that is validated through non–European norms and values.

13 Shahab Ahmed, *What is Islam?: The Importance of Being Islamic* (Princeton, NJ: Princeton University Press, 2015): 236.

14 I go on to say: "The focus on historical forces and social relations embeds an even greater departure from Islam viewed as universal religion with discrete beliefs, rituals and laws. To explore Islamicate civilization is to recognize and celebrate an Asian dimension in the lived experience of Muslim peoples... Most Muslims are Asian, and Islamicate civilization, like Muslim demography, derives its central focus, and determinative profile, from Asia." Bruce Lawrence, "Islamicate Civilization: The View from Asia" in Brannon M. Wheeler (ed.), *Teaching Islam* (New York, NY: Oxford University Press, 2003): 61–74, at 62 as quoted in Ahmed (2015): 172. While Islamicate remains distinct from, and analytically productive beyond, Muslim/Islamic elements in world history, one should expand the arc of influence to include Africa as a domain of Islamicate activity equally prized alongside the Asian narratives and evidence I highlight elsewhere.

15 Armando Salvatore, *The Sociology of Islam: Knowledge, Power and Civility* (Oxford: Wiley-Blackwell, 2016): 123–125, except for the bracketed definition of *adab* cited from p. 280. (Elsewhere, Salvatore further defines *adab* as "an elite-oriented yet flexible matrix of rules of good life, courteous exchange, and civic cohesion based on bundling together cultured life forms considered adequate to respond to Islam's core message without falling into the trap of considering it as a totalizing and closed doctrine." See *Wiley-Blackwell Companion to Islam* (Oxford: Wiley-Blackwell, 2016): 34.) Much more could be said of Salvatore's approach to Islam in general and his use of Hodgson in particular. His is perhaps the most thoroughgoing application of Hodgsonian approaches and terminology to a revisionist sociology of Islam. He notes that Hodgson's "majestic historical trilogy provides the main source for the sociology of Islam," especially during the Middle Periods (mid-10th to mid-15th centuries), and expresses his hope to make the 2016 book the first in a trilogy that would include *The Law, the State and the Public Sphere*

as also *Transnationalism, Transculturalism, and Globalization*, all major themes and contested topics that he discusses but only briefly in the 2016 monograph (p. xii).

16 Hodgson (1974) *The Venture of Islam*, vol. 2: 55n. The quote from Nile Green appears in his review of Robert Irwin, *Ibn Khaldun: An Intellectual Biography* (Princeton, NJ: Princeton University Press, 2018), where Irwin argues that Ibn Khaldun needs to be seen within a premodern or medieval lens and cannot be linked to global history or civilization studies. But Green, like Salvatore, sees him as a premodern scholar who is also a modern exemplar. There could not be two more dramatically opposite approaches to Ibn Khaldun than Salvatore (2016) and Irwin (2018), illustrating the importance of this 14th-century Maghribi theorist across centuries and continents.

17 For two recent works that highlight the Mediterranean as a distinct, yet undervalued, field of academic inquiry for comparative studies, see miriam cooke, Erdag Göknar, and Grant Parker, eds., *Mediterranean Passages: Readings from Dido to Derrida* (Chapel Hill, NC: University of North Carolina, 2008) and Brian A. Catlos and Sharon Kinoshita, eds., *Can We Talk Mediterranean? Conversations on an Emerging Field in Medieval and Early Modern Studies* (New York, NY: Palgrave-Macmillan, 2017).

18 For the first and fullest development of Ibn Khaldun as an *adib*, see miriam cooke, "Ibn Khaldun and Language: From Linguistic Habit to Philological Craft" in Bruce B. Lawrence, ed., *Ibn Khaldun and Islamic Ideology* (Leiden, Germany: Brill, 1984): 27–36. There is no single English equivalent of *adab*, and so I leave it untranslated, though earlier I did outline its features vis-à-vis *taskhir*.

19 See Bruce B. Lawrence, Introduction to Franz Rosenthal, tr., *The Muqaddimah: An Introduction to History*, abridged and edited by N.J. Dawood (Princeton, NJ: Princeton University Press, Bollingen Series, 1967/2005): xvi.

20 *Hadith* criticism is in effect the science of personality criticism (*'ilm al-jarh wal-ta'dil*). Though introduced at the outset of Book One of *Kitab al-'ibar* (Dawood, abridg., Rosenthal, tr., (1967/2005):35, n. 1), it is not fully explained till much later, requiring the reader to make explicit the connection that is left implicit by Ibn Khaldun. It needs to be underscored what was said earlier about Biruni: both

performed and advocated scientific knowledge, yet neither was strictly speaking a "scientist," but rather a "natural philosopher" engaged by empirical methodology as the surest means to pragmatic and trustworthy practices.

21 Abdesselam Cheddadi, *Actualite d'Ibn Khaldun: Conferences et Entretiens* (Temara, Morocco: Maison des Arts, des Sciences et des Lettres, 2006): 69 shows the importance of this category for Ibn Khaldun. I am indebted to Cheddadi for the citation (p. 69) as for many other insights into the mercurial, restless mind of Ibn Khaldun. I differ only in translating the Arabic phrase as "known world" (corresponding to Greek *ecumene*) rather than inhabited world, since the former suggests the connectedness of those distant parts, often port cities on islands or continents, that were more aware of a dispersed human community across the globe than were their neighbors living in remote inland regions.

22 For an explication of these three types of knowledge by another 20th-century Maghribi thinker, Muhammad 'Abid al-Jabiri, see the summary in Ali A. Allawi, *The Crisis of Islamic Civilization* (New Haven, CT: Yale University Press, 2010): 104–107. The book is replete with insight into dilemmas and challenges facing Muslim scholars, with apt critique of Wahhabi versions of Islamism, attention to Shi'ite exemplars, and a tilt toward Traditionalist and Perennialist thinkers, albeit mingled with criticism of some of its major exponents.

23 Allawi (2010): 72–73.

24 Walter Mignolo, *The Darker Side of Western Modernity: Global Futures, Decolonial Options* (Durham, NC: Duke University Press, 2011): 98.

25 Mignolo (2011).

4

Premodern Afro-Eurasia

To understand the longer diachronic scope of Islamicate/Persianate underpinnings to an Islamicate Cosmopolitan Spirit (ICS), we must revisit Hodgson's moral vision of world history. He thought that Islam mattered because it righted the intellectually wrong, but also emotively triumphalist, notions of Eurocentric domination in world history. The first correction is temporal: he expands the corridor of the past. He stressed the formative features of world civilization dating from three millennia before Christ. Already by the middle of the first millennium before the Common Era, there existed four cultural core areas: Mediterranean, Nile-to-Oxus, Indian, and East Asian (or Chinese). Two rivers, the Nile to the south and Oxus to the north, are the map markers etching the core area of Islamicate civilization. There is no Middle East or Near East, the mere invocation of which involves a presentist view of history, out of sync with developments that preceded "the rise of the West." It was two rivers, the Nile and the Oxus, and it is these two rivers which framed major developments characterizing the early three phases of Islamicate civilization

Here *in nuce* is what Hodgson argued about the importance of seeing Islam over the timeframe of 1,500 years but with an emplotment that was actually 2,500 years. World history is actually history of the ecumene, the known world, at once settled and connected. By the middle of the first millennium BCE, the ecumene had crystallized into four cultural core areas: Mediterranean, Nile-to-Oxus, Indic, and East Asian. The Nile-to-Oxus, the future core of Islamdom (another Hodgson neologism), was the least cohesive and the most complicated. Whereas each of the other regions developed a single language of high culture—Greek, Sanskrit, and Chinese, respectively—the Nile-to-Oxus region was a linguistic palimpsest of Irano-Semitic languages of several sorts: Aramaic, Syriac (eastern or Iranian Aramaic), and Middle Persian (the language of eastern Iran). The Nile-to-Oxus region, of course, became conjoined with the Arabian Peninsula through the expansion of early Muslim rule to neighboring regions, but the nature of the society, culture, and religion that evolved was bidirectional. Though the Arabs conquered, they were challenged and changed by the people, the institutions, and the societies they conquered.

Hodgson's vision resembles the earlier vision of the 14th-century polymath Ibn Khaldun. In his famed *Muqaddimah*,[1] Ibn Khaldun had argued that history was about social organization and civilizational patterns: religion mattered less for its heroes than for the patterns of social exchange that they promoted. In a similar vein, Hodgson locates Islam not as an outsider but an insider to world history, with more than religion at stake. Islam was so broad, its influence so pervasive, that it defies categorization as Muslim or Islamic, belonging only to Muslim actors and practices, creeds, rituals, or structures. Instead, for Hodgson, there is a vibrant, portable, resilient tradition that is best understood as Islamic*ate*. The -*ate* is much more than an added syllable: it is a stark challenge to rethink all that is meant by Muslim and Islam. It is the social and cultural palette that emerged from Muslim rule, encompassing and influencing non-Muslims as well as Muslims. Islamic*ate*, with the -*ate* tacked on to the end, adds oddity and resonance to what becomes the heritage of Islam for world civilization.

Underlying this central argument is an even larger premise: there is only one world civilization and Islam is a part of it, not apart from it. Islamicate tradition encompasses but also projects all the elements of Islamic thought that came from pre-Islamic resources—Persian, Hebrew, Greek, Latin, by language; Magian, Jewish, and Christian by religion; Byzantine, Sassanian, Mongol by imperial domains. Islamicate civilization becomes part and parcel of the spirit directed Westward in developments unfolding after 1800, but crucial to its expanse and durability for more than a millennium was the Persianate or Eastern hemispheric spirit.

The Persianate

The Persianate is no less important than Islamicate in considering the emergence of a cosmopolitan ethos within Islamdom. The two are inseparable. Persianate is itself a subset of Islamicate; the two neologisms are linked to a broadly revisionist project of seeing Islam as part of world history, exceptional in its scope but not in its nature, marking hemispheric connections across time and space. As Mana Kia has astutely observed, "Hodgson considers the Persianate as one form of the Islamicate, with Persian merely a language to express Islamicate concepts."[2] If Islamicate expands Islam to mean more than religion or Arab origins, Persianate reinforces Persian as more than the language of Iran or the special element of Shi'i Islam. It is not only possible but also necessary to speak of a Persianate core within the emergence of Islamicate civilization. Inherited from the Greeks was the notion of oikoumene, aka ecumene, the inhabited or civilized world, its nodes, whether coastal ports or inland cities, connected by trade and commerce, as also by conquest and war. For much of Islamicate history it was the impact of Persianate culture that etched major developments and provided durable legacies. Persianate is linked to Islamicate yet distinct from it, not least in its interaction with Turkic languages. "What was remarkable about the growth of the Persian literary medium," explains Abbas Amanat, "was its ability to adjust to new cultural settings, allowing in turn the production of an indigenous *belles lettres* or the *divan*-related literature. It coexisted and crossbred with the emerging Turkic languages and cultures in Anatolia, in the Caucasus and in Central Asia, and with the multilingualism of Hindustan." The process was aided and abetted by strife, war, and travel throughout the 11th–16th centuries, when "literary talents, poets, and 'men of the pen' roamed throughout a vast territory in search of patronage and fame outside of their homelands."[3]

Consider the migration of a central term/concept, *adab*, best rendered not just as literature but self-conscious moral monitoring, reflective deference, or polite behavior as the norm in all social encounters. In examining a range of sociocultural norms lumped together under the term "*adab*," one might use the qualifier Persianate, if one wants to stress the importance of Persian as a linguistic component, or Islamicate, if one wants to acknowledge the way in which Islam itself is invoked even when the connection between cultural observance and religious loyalty proves to be very slim. Persian poetry written by Turks, Persian paintings produced by Indians, Persian monumental architecture built by Mongols—all have Islamicate dimensions, yet are not restricted to a specific religious audience or to a precise ritual usage. Even when Persianate and Islamicate seem to converge, they express complementary excesses: Persianate connotes more than linguistic usage, just as Islamicate connotes more than creedal commitment, ritual performance, or juridical loyalty.

All dates are subjective, open to challenge and change, but the period from 900–1900 defines the impact of Persianate forces within Islamicate civilization. It is even possible to speak of a Persian(ate) cosmopolis, as one distinguished historian has argued. It was a transregional movement, originating in Iran as response to the 7th-century Arab conquests but encompassing far more than the boundaries of present-day Iran or the protocols of Shi'i Islam. To understand the depth and durability of the Persianate core within Islamicate civilization one needs to trace its contours. As Richard Eaton has eloquently demonstrated, Persians adopted Arabic calligraphy but changed its content. By the mid-10th century Persian writers in Khurasan— that is, northeastern Iran, western Afghanistan, and Central Asia— began appropriating the heritage of both Arab Islam and pre-Islamic

Iran; that is, they self-consciously included both cultural traditions, that of ancient Iran and that of 7th-century Arabia, in a new hybrid cultural idiom. It was supported by local courts but they straddled the Iranian plateau connecting with India to the south, Central Asia to the north, and China to the east (via the Silk Road). To explain how this was possible, one needs to conjure a radically cosmopolitan culture. It goes back to one region, Khurasan, and to its capital cities, first Merv, then later Nishapur, but above all, there was the intrinsic fluidity and diversity of its inhabitants. Its communities consisted of Jews, Christians, Manichaeans, Zoroastrians, Buddhists, pagans, and shamanists, together with both Shiʻite and Sunni Muslims. Not only did New Persian, as this language was called, become a common linguistic denominator in a multiethnic society, it also stood outside rather than within any tradition, whether ethnic or religious. Above all, New Persian posed no ideological threat to Arabic, the language of Iran's 7th-century Islamic victors, which is why Hodgson sometimes speaks of Perso-Arabic in describing elites who wrote in Arabic, even while using (New) Persian as their lingua franca.[4]

It is difficult to overstress the portability of this language, along with the culture and the moral conscience it conveyed. It was not devoid of political instrumentality; indeed, it served the goals and courts of many rulers throughout Central and South, and even Southeast Asia, from the 11th through the 19th centuries. It reinforced the idea that kingship was about more than conquest and power; it was also about moral justice as the basis of sovereignty, prosperity, and longevity. It even survived arguably the worst premodern disaster to afflict the Muslim world, the Mongol conquests of the 13th–15th centuries. Historians even speak of the Mongol holocaust that afflicted Iran, Central Asia, and North India. It was Persianate culture that many survivors of Mongol conquest carried with them to their new homes. Jalaluddin Rumi (d. 1273), the famed whirling dervish and author of the Persian class, *Mathnawi-e ma'navi*, settled in Anatolia but continued to write in Persian.

Eaton aptly summarizes this process of retention and diffusion for Persianate cosmopolitanism:

> Apart from political ideology, other components of the Persian cosmopolis diffused throughout India after the thirteenth century, including architecture, dress, courtly comportment, cuisine, and especially, lexicon. As the geographic reach of Persian letters expanded, so did the production of dictionaries, whose compilers endeavored to make literature produced in different parts of the Persophone world mutually comprehensible. From the 14th century dictionaries began to be produced in India, where such works rendered Persian equivalences for words not only in Indian languages, but also in Turkish, Pashto, Aramaic, Greek, Latin, and Syriac.
>
> *Indeed, between the 16th and 19th centuries, of all Persian language dictionaries produced anywhere, most were produced in India* [my emphasis]. From the 14th century on, Persian had become the most widely used language for governance across the subcontinent, as Indians filled the vast revenue and judicial bureaucracies in the Delhi sultanate and its successor states, and later in the Mughal empire (1526–1858) and its successor states.
>
> As a result, Persian terms infiltrated the vocabulary of nearly all major regional languages of South Asia. Vernaculars like Bengali or Telugu are replete with Persian terms pertaining not only to governance, but to commerce, literacy, cuisine, music, textiles, and technologies of all sorts.[5]

Perhaps the crucial element for this Persian cosmopolis was its ability to appropriate earlier prestigious and cosmopolitan cultures, whether from pre-Islamic Iran, ancient Greek, or contemporary Byzantine, Indic, and Chinese traditions. While it never neglected Arabic elements, especially the priority of the Qur'an as a religious text and the Prophet Muhammad as the model human, it exceeded the dictates of orthodoxy as also its limits. Indeed, as Eaton astutely observed, "it was precisely the non-religious character of this larger Persian cosmopolis that allowed non-Muslims to readily assimilate so many of its aspects" but also allowed Muslims of diverse persuasions and practices to embrace its moral and aesthetic values.[6]

51

Other scholars, less focused on the Asian subcontinent than Eaton, have taken note of the expansiveness of a Persian cosmopolis, marked by a Persianate spirit that was at once cosmopolitan and Islamicate. In the new journal series titled *Journal of Persianate Studies*, dating back to 2008, its chief editor, the noted sociologist Saïd Amir Arjomand, declared:

> The Persianate civilizational area includes India and therefore its study cuts across the arbitrary division that has developed institutionally between Middle Eastern and South Asian area studies. The Persianate world also includes Central Asia, the study of which was orphaned until the demise of the Soviet Union, and has more recently been relegated to a number of separate learned societies. Persian also became the lingua franca of several kingdoms and empires in the eastern Muslim lands and thus formed the nucleus of a vast civilizational area which we call the Persianate world.
>
> The unity of the Persianate world [notes Arjomand] was undermined with the rise of Western imperialism in the nineteenth century, and shattered by the creation of nation states in the twentieth. Under the impact of British imperialism, Persian literacy gradually became a nostalgic veneer in India. Although Persian remained a living language in Central Asia under Russian and Soviet imperialism, it was increasingly cut off from the Iranian nation-state, the core Persianate society in the twentieth century.

Yet revival of a Persianate ethos is still possible, at least within the academy since:

> Techno-scientific globalization, as well as the disintegration of the Soviet empire and the opening of Afghanistan, and visible cracks in the edifice of state-formation and its exclusionary, nationalistic political culture, all open new possibilities for symbiosis within the Persianate world and thus for the development of Persianate studies. It is into this newly opened cultural space that the Association for the Study of Persianate Societies has inserted itself; and it is this cultural space, the field of interdisciplinary Persianate studies, that our Journal intends to cover.[7]

Other initiatives to expand Persianate studies, and also the greater circuit of Islamicate influences, will be reviewed in the final chapter. What is crucial to note is that the Persian cosmopolis, like Islamdom generally, is neither unified nor united but instead proliferating and decentering. It does not belong solely to Iran or Iranians. It is at once centrifugal and vernacular, defined as a style more than a regime, a performance rather than a conformity.

And so, one must ask: why it has taken so long to produce, then disseminate, and now reproduce and expand a Persianate dimension within Islamdom? While the durability under stress of these cultural resources from the Afro-Eurasian ecumene is notable, there are multiple factors that marred its initiation and to continue to inhibit its expansion. Some derive from European geo-politics, but others arise within Islamdom as also Euro-American academia. All need to be reviewed, assessed, and put into perspective.

Decline But Not Defeat of Persianate Accents in Islamicate Civilization

There were twin causes, separate in origin but convergent in impact, for the decline of Persianate accents in the early modern Islamicate world. One was the preemptive nature of European colonial rule, what Arjomand calls, "the rise of Western imperialism." Not only did English replace Persian as the language of bureaucracy in British India but also it did so with a markedly prejudicial motif. In 1837, English superseded Persian as the official language of the Company, in large part because one of its major officials, Macaulay, was influenced by Bentinck's philosophy of utilitarianism (to wit, only what is pragmatically useful not what is morally right or aesthetically engaging that should be the object of education). Macaulay played a major role in introducing English and Western concepts to education in India. He supported the replacement of Persian by English as the official language, the use of English as the medium of instruction in all schools, and the training of English-speaking Indians as teachers. Persian was still used by Muslim elites (including the poets Ghalib and Iqbal) but lost its currency in the Anglo-oriented and British dependent sectors of colonial India.

Yet there was more than British imposition of English as an imperial language that undercut Persian in India. At the same time as Persian receded in India, especially but not solely in the areas under British rule, *it was challenged by indigenous movements for greater reliance on "native" languages.* Hence in South Asia, Hindi written in Sanskrit script challenged Urdu in Persian script, each taking on the color of partisan groups defined by region, ethnicity, and increasingly (after 1860) religion.[8] Elsewhere in Central Asia Turkic ascendancy marked the 19th century. An apt example comes from the regions of Central Asia bordering present-day China. In Xinjiang and Kyrgyzstan, one can detect and trace several examples of how Turkic cultural nationalisms over the past century have successfully dethroned Persianate culture from its valued role as language of education, literacy, and religious tradition.[9] These efforts reflect political and personal efforts to manage culture and place it within national frames studded with symbols of descent from a purified past. Romantic nationalist narratives of elite–commoner divides have helped redefine cultural exchange as the source of deleterious pollution carried by deracinated cosmopolitan intellectuals.

Already in the pre-Mongol period in Islamic Central Asia, Turkic authors were competing with Persians to claim some of the cultural status attained by the latter within the Islamic world, but mostly on the margins of what was still a dominant Persianate culture among elites. Self-conscious Turkic ethno-cultural nationalism before the modern period is hard to trace, but it is possible to see how some modern Turkic scholars do appreciate the accomplishments and influences of Persianate culture, yet radically redefine them since there is little political tolerance for public discussions about a Turko-Persianate cosmopolitan past. As a result, contemporary observers should see the highly plural Turko-Persian societies not as syntheses so much as mosaics. That is not to deny their cosmopolitan past, but simply to acknowledge that many pieces of these mosaics did not become ethnically distinct until rearranged and revalued within modern nation states to reinvent separate traditions. In short, the Persianate, a marker of *barzakh* logic, has been suppressed and redirected as part of a primordial past with "borders," one absent the markers of "foreign" influence.

Added to these factors, and abetted by them, is a failure of the cosmopolitan imagination not just among politicians and pragmatists but also among scholars projecting national values even while claiming a larger, transnational mandate. This process is especially evident in museum catalogues. Let me just provide one example evident from modern-day Turkey in one of the most sophisticated of the new museums that dot the Istanbul skyline. It comes from a museum catalogue that traces political aestheticism from the 11th–18th-century Muslim world. Titled *3 Capitals of Islamic Art*, it features objects from the Louvre collection in Paris on display in Istanbul at Sakıp Sabancı Müzesi in 2008. Its aim is to highlight the artistic production of three metropolitan sites in the premodern Muslim world: Istanbul, Isfahan, and Delhi (Figure 4.1).

All three capital cities—Istanbul, Isfahan, and Delhi—were influenced by Persian but also Chinese and Central Asian motifs. To understand their confluence, in my view, requires recognizing the Timurid origins of what I call embedded cosmopolitanism. It was embedded because it was represented by artifacts less than by explicit analysis. It depended on urban trade networks that shaped and reshaped aesthetic norms and cultural production throughout the Afro-Eurasian ecumene. Only Hodgson hints at their collective connection to Timur/Tamerlane (d. 1405), a Chaghatai Turk with Mongol aspirations. Hodgson renames the Mughal dynasty as Indo-Timurid, that is, Timur in India, since Babur, its founder, was the great great great grandson of Tamerlane. Proud of his ancestry, Babur, like Timur, had no Mongol blood, only Mongol attachment. To simply label Timur a Turkic Muslim is to underestimate and so undervalue the huge cultural heritage, the Mongol ethos, that extends back to his distant ancestry.[11]

Figure 4.1   3 Capitals of Islamic Art.
Source: Louvre Collection

What makes all three empires Islamicate? Because they are not just linked to Timur but also to a certain sensibility. All three are post-Timurid empires: in addition to kingship and sainthood, they embrace a public celebratory tone—at once aesthetic and ethical—in everyday life. To quote from the catalogue: "The three Islamic empires of this exhibition, Ottoman (1299–1923), Safavid (1501–1722) and Mughal (1526–1858), shared a common cultural heritage forged by the former Islamic dynasties of the geographic region of premodern Greater Iran (parts of Transoxiana, Afghanistan, Iran and Iraq), the last propagators of which are the Timurids (1396–1510)." And then because constructed notions of national identity intrude, modern sensibility accepts the Safavids as the natural heirs of the former dynasties of Iran (the modern state) for territorial reasons, even though the Mughals, whose dynastic founder

(Babur) was the grandson of Timur himself, had close family ties to Timur and considered themselves carriers of Persianate culture. The Ottoman case is absent territorial or genealogical ties, yet Istanbul shares common affinity with Isfahan and Delhi because all three empires share moral and aesthetic values: kingship embodies not just hierarchy but also justice, and beyond sovereignty art reflects empathetic engagement with nature, with animal and aviary life, but especially with tulips. Together literature and art project, the distinctive ethos of an ICS.[12]

Consider a 16th-century Iznik plate. Here tulips triumph, as they do in both Turkey and Iran from the premodern to the modern to the contemporary period (Figure 4.2):

But the best way to describe this diffuse and popular pattern is not Muslim, though there are Muslim consumers, nor Islamic, though many see an engagement with Qur'anic themes of nature and balance. This pattern instead projects Islamicate taste, or better an

Figure 4.2   Iznik plate.
Source: Louvre—Plat aux tulipes

ICS, because it permeates all levels of society, from Syria to Turkey to China. "The local production of tiles," as the catalogue explains, "were known in Damascus as '*qishani*' derived from the name of the Iranian city of Kashan (because they were linked to that site), until the nineteenth century." Its historical and geographical origins are deeper still, however, for "the Damascene color palette is a color scheme already found in the Mamluk era, its blue-white contrasts reflecting the concern to imitate Chinese Yuan and Ming porcelain." Indeed, the primary difference between Iznik plates of the late 15th century and earlier Damascene tiles is that the technology of the former "brought the quality of Iznik production on a par with that of Chinese porcelain and contributed to their international renown, which endures to this day."[14]

What needs to be stressed here is overlapping networks—their extent, their antiquity, and their consequence. In porcelain art, there is a huge transregional network of both production and aesthetic taste that originated from the Yuan (Mongol) period and persisted through Timur (a Chaghatai Turk as well as a Mongol in his ancestry), and shaped the public as well as private taste of those who were its most avid consumers. And nowhere is this arc of influence—at once territorially and culturally capacious—more evident than in poetry. Not just the art but also the verse can/should be described as Islamicate and, to the extent that it echoed the influence of Greater Iran, Persianate. Here we find Islamicate/Persianate lyrics linking Iran to Syria to Turkey. That is, they display Turko-Arab-Persian taste, with Mongol-Central Asian antecedents, in the form of Syrian Ottoman Persianate tile. It occupied domestic space in 16th-century Damascus (Figure 4.3).

In the catalogue, we are simply told that "the panel displays the final beyt of a ghazal by the famous poet Hafiz, a native of the city of Shiraz: 'The chant of Thy assembly swells the heavens, now that the poem of Hafiz of mellifluous tongue is Thy song.'" Yet, as the cataloguer goes on to explain, "this panel does not come from Iran, but in all likelihood from Syria." And what are its aesthetic characteristics? "In the floriated frieze framing the inscription can be seen

Figure 4.3 Hafiz plate from Damascus.
Source: Sabanci Museum

the bright chrome green so characteristic of Damascence production in the Ottoman era, combined with cobalt blue and turquoise" (and one might also add, with a dominant blue-white contrast harking back to the rivalry/emulation of Chinese tiles).[15]

The examples could be multiplied but their collective impact is to underscore the nature of a pervasive Islamicate/Persianate cosmopolitan taste.[16] It exceeded religion, but also embodied its universal values. It exceeded region yet claimed the mantle of authentic local culture. It exceeded language: neither Arabic nor Turkish but "new" Persian, it projected an idiom—at once written, heard, recited, and often sung—inclusive of Islamdom, the premodern world inhabited by Muslims and non-Muslims, mostly under the rule of Muslim emperors. If none of this is evident to the cataloguer, it is not because s/he has a deficient education or a limited worldview, it is because within the modern-day Republic of Turkey, no less than its Turkic neighbors in Central Asia, it is difficult to recuperate the cosmopolitan past, one that is a Turko-Persianate cultural past, one not reducible to an ethnically distinct, and allegedly superior, Turkic heritage.

This double outlook—at once cosmopolitan yet national, invoking the past while also redefining its importance—makes it especially hard to speak of cosmopolitanism in 21st-century Turkey. The challenge has been etched in local detail by Amy Mills, an American ethnographer. She looks at Istanbul through a broad, postcolonial optic. She recognizes the fiction of dividing history in general and

Middle East history in particular into regions, polities, and states that experienced or did not experience colonial rule. Even though Istanbul was never colonized on the ground, its inhabitants were shaped by European expansion, not least the remapping of Afro-Asian territories from the 18th century on.

Mills' special focus is on the role of minorities. Without attention to the role and the status of minorities, she argues, one cannot make any claims about cosmopolitan practices or legacy.[17] But there is a special role for minorities in the consideration of Islamicate cosmopolitan: Post-Ottoman Empire nodes of local cosmopolitan ethos are found in areas where mixed communities live side-by-side, or where the memories of those moments engage those who are its heirs. It is not solely about counting residents, or doing a census of neighbors; there must also be a passion for the beauty of what was mingled and mixed, enduring beyond every experiment at unmixing, whether racial or ethnic, linguistic or religious, separation of parts and persons.

Yes, minorities are important, but not as minorities so much as catalysts and registers of difference that permeate the fabric of what becomes the social palimpsest of genuinely, deeply, and irrevocably pluralist societies. In the case of the Ottoman Empire, Greeks and Kurds, Armenians, Circassians, and Jews—all count as major elements of the past, even when they are few or minuscule in the current profile of the Republic of Turkey.

The actual history of minorities in Turkey belies their residual importance for cosmopolitan logic. During the collapse of the Ottoman Empire, all indigenous minorities came to be redefined as potential compradors, agents of outside forces. Their historical past was reshaped by their symbolic link to European others. After the founding of the Turkish Republic in 1923, notes Mills, Jews and Christians "were seen both as betrayers of the Turkish nation-state and as uncomfortable reminders of the Ottoman imperial past." Instead of a cosmopolitan embrace, these minorities experienced a nationalist rebuff. Christian and Jewish minorities were granted formal legal equality in Turkey, but in practice they experienced discrimination that forced thousands to leave Turkey during the past century.[18]

The result in Istanbul alone is dramatic. At the turn of the 20th century, non-Muslim minorities and foreigners constituted 56% of the city's population, but "by the end of the 20th century, after massive minority emigration and the rural-urban migration of Kurds and Turks to Istanbul, Christians and Jews constituted less than 1 percent of the population of a city of more than 10 million people."[19] (Today, in 2020, the population has increased to 16 million, Jews and Christians of all denominations number less than 100,000, closer to 0.5% of the total.)

Cosmopolitanism in early 21st-century Istanbul becomes the equivalent of a polite historical fig leaf: it reveals what it pretends to conceal. "In Istanbul," concludes Mills, "cosmopolitanism is imagined locally in ways that perpetuate the notions of social difference and inequality that cosmopolitanism, as an ideal, claims to transcend."[20] But because memories persist, they fuel the tension between belonging—to the Republic of Turkey as a national citizen—and longing—to be part of the Ottoman past as a cosmopolitan subject. More than just a population downshift for minorities there is the struggle among Stamboulites to advocate difference, even against the tide of change that Mills has so carefully and nimbly documented. ICS persists as an ideal even when its memories are tarnished by adverse historical changes.

Notes

1 His fame now extends to the Internet age. See Richard Feloni, "Why Mark Zuckerberg Wants Everyone to Read the 14th Century Islamic Book 'the Muqaddimah'," *Business Insider* (June 2, 2015) at http://uk.businessinsider.com/mark-zuckerberg-the-muqaddimah-2015-6?r=US.

2 Mana Kia, *Persianate Selves: Memories of Place and Origin before Nationalism* (Stanford, CA: Stanford University Press, 2020): 14.

3   Abbas Amanat, "Remembering the Persianate" in Abbas Amanat and Assef Ashraf, *The Persianate World: Rethinking a Shared Sphere* (Leiden/Boston, MA: Brill, 2019): 34. "Hindustan" is the Persian name to describe the Indian subcontinent.

4   For much of the analysis that follows, I am indebted to Richard M. Eaton and his deft exposition of Persianate antecedents, developments, and challenges in an article, "Revisiting the Persian Cosmopolis," *Asia Times* (July 19, 2014). See http://www.atimes.com/ atimes/South_Asia/SOU-01-190713.html, no longer extant but available at https://www.gcgi.info/blog/423-revisiting-the-persian-cosmopolis-the-world-order-and-the-dialogue-of-civilisations. The essay anticipates, and is now superseded by, Eaton's recent monograph, *India in the Persianate Age 1000–1765* (London: Penguin, 2019). This monograph is especially notable for its reassessment of south India at the intersection of two cosmopolises: Persian and Sanskrit: "a deeper trend in the Deccan's cultural history, namely a progressive interpenetration of the Sanskrit and Persianate worlds between the fourteenth and sixteenth centuries" (pp. 457–458). Later, the great Mughals facilitated the formation of a transregional empire with the "circulation of people along established transregional networks that connected key centres of Persianate cultural production" (p. 901). The denouement of the early modern period is also marked by literary indices: "Between the mid eighteenth and the late nineteenth centuries, two great transregional languages, which for centuries had defined the Sanskritic and Persianate worlds, became artefacts in India, eclipsed in the north by new literary genres in dialects of spoken Hindavi – prominently Braj and Urdu. And yet, although the patronage of Sanskrit and Persian literature and the usage of the two languages receded dramatically, the values, sentiments and ideas sustained through their respective literary traditions had become deeply enmeshed over the course of nearly a millennium of mutual interaction" (pp. 922–923). It is hard to imagine a more expansive narrative of the Persianate tradition in South Asia than Eaton here provides.

5   See Eaton (2004) "Revisiting the Persian Cosmopolis" cited above.

6   For a further engagement with the stability and expansion of Persian literary conventions throughout eastern Islamdom, from the 9th to the 19th century, including China, see Brian Spooner and William

L. Hanaway, eds., *Literacy in the Persianate World: Writing and the Social Order* (Philadelphia, PA: University of Pennsylvania Museum of Archaeology and Anthropology, 2012). On the basis of more than 30 years of archaeological and textual studies, Victor Mair concludes that: "the Iranian peoples (i.e., speakers of Iranian languages) were the paramount *Kulturvermittlers* (culture brokers/transmitters) of Eurasia from the Bronze Age through the late medieval period" (p. 389). Not only was Persian prominent and the art of writing Persian preserved among Chinese Muslims but Persian continues to be taught in contemporary China (p. 404).

7   Saïd Amir Arjomand, "Defining Persianate Studies," *Journal of Persianate Studies* I (2008), 3–4. I have omitted part of the defense of this new journal and altered the last sentence to clarify the author's intent. Also notable is Arjomand's subsequent overview assessment of Hodgson in *Encyclopaedia Iranica*. See Saïd Amir Arjomand, "HODGSON, MARSHALL GOODWIN SIMMS," *Encyclopædia Iranica*, online edition, 2015. Available at http://www.iranicaonline.org/articles/hodgson-marshall (accessed November 14, 2020). Arjomand's judgment that "Islamicate" has become a widely accepted term is questionable, but his staging of Hodgson's historical revisionism is astute and laudable.

8   For an excellent assessment of Persian or Indo-Persian in British India, despite the competition with Hindi-Urdu and the ascent of English, see Michael H. Fisher, "Teaching Persian as an Imperial Language in India and in England During the Late 18th and Early 19th Centuries" in Spooner/Hanaway (2012): 328–358.

9   In what follows I am indebted to Nathan Light, "Forgetting and Unbraiding: From Turko-Persianate Culture to Ethno-National Identities," an abstract he submitted for the Yale conference on the Persianate World (May 9–11, 2014). The book subsequently published from that conference—Abbas Amanat and Assef Ashraf, eds., *The Persianate World: Rethinking a Shared Sphere* (Leiden, the Netherlands: Brill, 2019)—does not include a chapter from Light. His website lists him as a folklorist and anthropologist who "investigates Uyghur and Kyrgyz practices in relation to temporality, heritage, sociality, communication, and technology." In a comprehensive

history of Persianate frontiers, Uyghur and Kyrgyz evidence fills an important Asian link.

10   Carol LaMotte, ed., *Istanbul, Isfahan, Delhi: Three of Islamic Art, Masterpieces from the Louvre Collection* (Istanbul: Sakip Sabanci Müzesi, 2008): front cover.

11   For the moral underpinning of monumental art for Babur's successor, Humayun, not least in his architectural choices, see the valuable essay by James Wescoat, Jr., "'In the Centre of the Map…': Reflecting on Marshall Hodgson's Ideas about Conscience and History in the Architectural Experience of Humayun," *South Asian Studies* 35(1) (2019), 7–24.

12   Some of these themes have been revisited and expanded in Mana Kia, *Persianate Selves: Memories of Place and Origin Before Nationalism* (Stanford, CA: Stanford University Press, 2020). The book appeared too late to be woven into my own narrative about Persianate longing, but this passage captures the tone of my argument: "Before nationalism, Persianate selves could hail from many places, and their origins comprised a variety of lineages. The interrelations among these lineages render coherent their multiple modes of imagination, practice, and experience," and the linchpin of this multiplicity, harking back to the poet Hafiz, was *adab*, "the proper form of things, as the means and manifestation of the most harmonious, beautiful, and virtuous substance, most perfect and closest to the Truth." In short, *adab* evoked and embodied both Persianate as well as Islamicate vistas of the transcendent (pp. 70–71).

13   LaMotte (2008): 131.

14   Charlotte Maury, "Iznik Ceramics and Tiles" in LaMotte (2008): 73.

15   For the image and commentary, see LaMotte (2008): 153. I am grateful to Christianne Gruber for two further references to Chinese porcelain and its impact on Islamicate art. Lisa Golombek, *Tamerlane's Tableware: A New Approach to the Chinoiserie Ceramics of Fifteenth- and Sixteenth-Century Iran* (Costa Mesa, CA: Mazda Press, 1996) and Yuka Kadoi, *Islamic Chinoiserie: The Art of Mongol Iran* (Edinburgh: Edinburgh University Press, 2009). I am also grateful to an outside reviewer for reference to the centrality of turquoise in the material production of these transcultural pieces of Islamicate art. See Arash Khazeni, *Sky Blue Stone: The Turquoise Trade in World History* (Berkeley,

CA: University of California Press, 2014). Khazeni provides the rare feat of tracing a single item and evaluating the cultural importance of blue that it embodied across borders—temporal and physical—in Islamicate civilization.

16 For several more examples, cited in a 2014 public talk at the Franklin Institute of the Humanities, see https://humanitiesfutures.org/papers/islamicate-cosmopolitan-past-without-future-future-still-unfolding (accessed June 14, 2020).

17 The argument about minorities as exemplars but also victims of cosmopolitan thinking is one to which we will return in Chapter 5, looking at evidence from Southeast Asia, but here it is applied with analytical rigor to Turkey, especially during the past century.

18 Amy Mills, *Streets of Memory: Landscape, Tolerance, and National Identity in Istanbul* (Athens, GA: University of Georgia Press, 2010): 8.

19 Mills (2010): 10.

20 Mills (2010): 211.

5

Persianate Culture Across the Indian Ocean

When we look beyond Istanbul and the Mediterranean, and survey the Indian Ocean, it is helpful to recall why *barzakh* logic helps rethink religion and culture. Shahab Ahmed, despite his many insights into the nature of language and the use of key words in defining Islam, fell short in overloading the word "Islamic." For Ahmed, both religion and culture as analytical categories collapsed into meaning making. Since Islamic could and should refer to culture as well as religion, there was no need, he argued, to use the term Islamicate instead of Islamic. In a prolonged analysis of my own use of Hodgson's qualifier, Ahmed states:

> When we say that to study Islamicate is to allow for the admission of Asia as an Islamicate variable, this seems to imply that if we want to study Islam—that is Islam-proper, Islam as religion, Islam as invariable—Asia is somewhat more dispensable. It is as if the only way to enfranchise the Muslims of Asia—who, at the latest reckoning are 62% of the Muslim population of the planet—is in the capacity of constituents of the Islamicate; their qualification as constituents for Islam is altogether more tenuous. Lawrence's utilization of Hodgson's concepts maneuvers us into a position where Asia is, by definition, simply not central to the constitution of Islam—it is only derivative/Islamicate.[1]

Islamicate Cosmopolitan Spirit, First Edition. Bruce B. Lawrence.
© 2021 Bruce B. Lawrence. Published 2021 by John Wiley & Sons, Ltd.

My argument is actually the opposite, that both religion and culture are fungible concepts, subject to *barzakh* logic: each elides with and often redefines the other but is never subsumed by its other. The position I am arguing against is one that posits a radical dichotomy between religion and culture. Since religion, like culture, is inseparable from language, I assert that a linguistic dyad of cultural identity defines Islam from the foundational period. It is not Arabic or Persian but at the same time it is *both* Persian and Arabic, like the very word *barzakh*, a Persian loanword in the Arabic Qur'an. Hodgson referred to the bilingual, but also bicultural, nature of Muslim identity as Irano-Semitic or Perso-Arabic. He coined the word Persianate to distinguish what he called the high culture of the expanding seams of Muslim empires from the 8th–18th centuries, and it included Asia, or better the Afro-Eurasian ecumene, as the heart and soul of Islamicate civilization.

The purpose of this chapter is to explore how Persianate became integral to Islamicate, while still retaining its own, distinctive trajectory, not least in that domain of the Afro-Eurasian ecumene that extends beyond the Iranian heartland, as also its adjacent regions, Central and South Asia, encompassing both East Africa and the Indian Ocean.

My argument begins with the status of Arabic. I argue that the literary preeminence of Arabic as the language of Qur'an, hadith, and Muslim religious scholarship conceals the Persianate substratum of almost all major markers of Islamicate civilization, from as early as the 8th, and certainly through the 18th century, of the Common Era. My further claim is that to understand the so-called peripheries of the Muslim world in 2020, we need to look at the radical vernaculars of local performance of Islam in Mayotte (southeast Africa) as also the visual publics that monitor transnational Islam in Indonesia. In sum, I have a two-part thesis: (1) that Islamicate civilization is more radically multicultural today than at any point in its past, but (2) to understand that florescence we have to begin with the axial moment of Irano-Semitic or Perso-Arabic origins in the earliest centuries of the Islamic era.

While Islam as religion has been often identified with the Arabic language and Arab norms, Arabs were merely the initiating agents for the development of Islamicate civilization. It was Persians, and even more Persianate norms, that provided the major instrument in premodern Muslim learning. What Arabs began Persians continued, but also modified.

It was no less a person than the Arab Prophet Muhammad who once observed: "If scholarship hung suspended in the highest parts of heaven, the Persians would attain it."[2] So evident was this Tradition to the universal historian Ibn Khaldun that he quoted it in the late 14th century in order to support his own observation, to wit, that "only the Persians have engaged in the task of preserving knowledge and writing systematic scholarly works."[3]

Just as the Arabic language was not limited to Arabs, having been mastered and used by Berbers, by Persians, and by Turks, among others, so Persian was not a language only for inhabitants of the Iranian plateau. From Central to South to Southeast Asia, Persian was used as both a literary and cultural idiom for diverse groups. Its flexibility as well as its appeal are better etched in the related but not identical term "Persianate."[4]

While Persianate depicts a cultural force linked both to the Persian language and to self-identified Persians, Persianate is more than either a language or a people; it highlights elements that Persians share with other non-Persian Muslims. Persianate is allied with Islamicate, and both relate to *adab*. Often rendered as custom in the broadest sense, *adab* is much more an ethical than a juridical concept. As Salvatore noted, *adab* derives from "the rules of courtly behavior 'courtesy', inspired by a sense of what is proper and beautiful."[5] *Adab* helps to illustrate the similarity of Islamicate/Persianate while also underscoring their nonequivalence. In examining a range of sociocultural norms lumped together under the term *adab*, one might use the qualifier Persianate, if one wants to stress the importance of Persian as a linguistic component, or Islamicate, if one wants to acknowledge the way in which Islam itself is invoked even when the connection between cultural observance and religious loyalty proves to be very slim. Persian poetry written by Turks, Persian paintings produced by Indians, Persian monumental architecture built by Mongols—all have Islamicate dimensions yet they are not restricted to a specific religious audience or to a precise ritual usage. Even when Persianate and Islamicate seem to converge, they express complementary excesses: Persianate connotes more than linguistic usage, just as Islamicate connotes more than creedal commitment, ritual performance, or juridical loyalty.

What becomes evident only from a Persianate rereading of Islamicate civilization is that Islam is neither acultural nor unicultural in its formation but radically multilinguistic and pluricultural. Hodgson, while prescient, was far too sophisticated in his rethinking of Islam in world history.[6] Few have followed in his footsteps to advance his insights and to apply his terminology to the range of cultures where Islam has dominated at the same time that local expressions have altered its practice. Both Mayotte in southeast Africa and Aceh in Southeast Asia represent contrasting case instances of the Islamicate template at work. Both examples are drawn from essays by field anthropologists, providing instances that amplify, and also corroborate, a crosscultural, multilingual approach to Islam in practice.

Michael Lambek, working in Mayotte, an island off of southeast Africa, has observed that "texts by themselves are silent: they become socially relevant through their enunciation, through citation, through acts of reading, reference, and interpretation. Therefore, we need to examine how texts are used and by whom, when recourse is made to textual authority, and what kinds of entailments such actions bring. Unless we view Islam in practice as well as in structure we cannot account for its relation to social organization or power, for the manner in which it both constitutes order and is in turn continuously regranted the authority to do so."

In order "to discover local hermeneutics," Lambek is led to look at the fringes of religious practice: texts that are used for magical purposes, and these are not easily deciphered. He notes how: "An emphasis on illocutionary acts allows us to approach the ostensibly 'magical' use of texts in a new light... Wearing Koranic verses and astrological symbols sewn into amulets and tied around the neck or waist forms a kind of continuous 'illocutionary' act, though the purification or protection is accomplished through a statement in writing rather than in speech... Likewise, the common medicine (used, for example, against the 'evil eye,' *dzitzu*) in which a verse from the Koran is written on a white plate, rinsed off, and then swallowed is a direct way of infusing the body with the sacred liturgy, yet another kind of embodiment of the text and a textualization, hence sanctification, of the body."[7]

What is never at stake is the certain knowledge of the texts. They are sacred; they embody truth, correction, guidance for humans within their orb of influence, but this same certain knowledge has to be transmitted, it has to become active, productive truth through individuals, and their performance leads to contestable authority because of "social organization" and also cultural preference. Through the instance of the Mayotte debate about Friday prayer, one is led to see how two forms of legitimacy—textual and social, or religious and cultural—coexist within a single manifestation of Islam, despite the tension between them at a particular historical moment. This case actually illustrates what Shahab Ahmed means by "convergent contradictions," but it does so by looking at different notions of authority in tension yet dialogue with one another. What we see are people engaged in dialogue in which personal and scriptural authority each play a part: they become subjects for debate but also the means by which positions in the debate are staked out and evaluated. Though the Arabic text is a starting point, it does not become a fixed boundary for Mayotte Muslim practitioners of magic; fuzzy or *barzakh* logic provides its own magical meaning, and so expands the horizon of possibility for the Islamicate cosmopolitan in her local context.

If Mayotte provides a southeast African vignette for Islamicate Cosmopolitan Spirit (ICS), illustrating why Islamicate cosmopolitan is always *spirit*, never fixed or reified, another vignette comes from Southeast Asia. A similar dialectic between the text and the context, the written word and the performance of its reception, takes place on the far side of the Indian Ocean in Indonesia, notably in the work of the Achinese artist A.R. Pirous. The anthropologist Kenneth M. George writes about Pirous in a masterful article titled: "Ethics, Iconoclasm, and Qur'anic Art in Indonesia."[8] Art, as George notes, is above all an ethical project, where one begins with the performer and then relates him/her to the residual grid of emotive, affective norms/values that never leave him or her. Aziz al-Azmeh sets the tone for what George wants to argue, to wit, that "like other religions, Islam is not a generic essence but a nominal entity that conjoins, by means of a name, a variety of societies, cultures, histories, and polities."[9] Yet there remains an affective core to what counts as Islamicate. For while there is no timeless theology of images, there is a range of emotions: aesthetic appreciation, awe, fascination, and revulsion. And they function as comportment, or self-expression (*adab*). Indeed, one could suggest, as Hirschkind has, that there is "the Quranically attuned body and soul," since Muslims in local contexts cultivate and attribute meaning to both body and soul, that is, to themselves.[10]

It was the Indonesian ulama who were the first anywhere to lodge protest against Pirous and their protest was picked up and reported by the press worldwide. The French designer pleaded ignorance as to the Qur'anic origin of the offending phrase. Eventually the rector of the Muslim Institute in Paris accepted his apology, and the ruckus, unlike the Rushdie Affair of 1989 or the Dutch Cartoons of 2006, or the Florida Qur'an burning threat of 2010, calmed down.

But what this episode illustrates is the proliferation of authority on a different scale than the Mayotte Muslim communities' debate about amulets or Friday prayer. While Islamic practice is deeply enmeshed in culture, the limits of cultural expression for Islamic truth—in this case, Qur'anic verses—is mediated not by artists but by trained clergy or groups that seek to speak as monitors of acceptable Muslim "art," whether produced by Muslims or non-Muslims. "Muslim art publics do not restrict their interests to the works and projects of Muslim artists alone," observes George, "but take it upon themselves to weigh in on the visual arts whenever they impinge on religious concerns. Indeed, these authorities and art publics are enmeshed in transnational networks of solidarity and debate, such that they may not only view themselves as part of a global Islamic community, but also seek a platform to speak for its interests or to act on behalf of the common good of Muslims everywhere. The Achinese painter A.D. Pirous, for instance, self-monitored himself and his recreation of Arabic calligraphy with Qur'anic precedents or models, for Pirous has always had to work in light of this popular fetishization of Arabic in which every instance of Arabic writing is construed as sacral, or as the Qur'an itself. Attitudes like this perhaps assure that Pirous's calligraphic paintings will be greeted with some reverence, but they also place his artworks at risk of public scrutiny by self-appointed scripturalists."[11]

And this observation, both by the artist himself and his several publics, takes on added significance in Indonesia because Arabic is not the language of everyday culture or social/political expression. Everywhere there are what George calls *the twin lives of Qur'anic signs*. They live as scripture and liturgical markers, but they also have a public, cultural life, and in that second use Quranic verses become more viral in producing anxieties in Southeast Asia because Arabic is a language set apart from, and above, local language/culture/religion. Relative to Indonesia, anxieties over Arabic orthography in places like Egypt or the non-Arab states of Iran and Pakistan are more relaxed for nearly everyone uses it in everyday communication. In Southeast Asia the hypersensitivity to Arabic as art is heightened by self-appointed vigilantes for Islamic purity. And that cultural difference is what underscores the Indonesian protest over the Achinese artist's effort to render Qur'anic verses into calligraphic paintings. In Indonesia's art public, as in Islamic communities and networks more broadly, observes George, the principal and most vocal authorities on Qur'anic art are religious elites who have very little background in the arts but who figure centrally in the visual culture surrounding the Qur'an. As the leading custodial authorities on Qur'anic matters, it is they who are most anxious about guarding the sanctity of the Qur'an and preserving Qur'anic Arabic as an unblemished verbal sign. It is they who are most ideologically invested in keeping

Qur'anic Arabic a religious concern, and putting a check to any expressive or pictorial manipulations of the Qur'an for worldly ends. But they need to be ever vigilant because the realm of culture is at once so porous and so inviting.

Perhaps the most graphic example of testing the limits of Arabic as a popular icon with porous boundaries in Indonesia is the case of the performance artist, Arahmaiani. Here she is holding a plate with the name Allah written on it in Arabic (Figure 5.1).

More than just another creative project, the Allah plate is intended to raise a crucial, oft-ignored perspective: there is no normative ethics for works of Muslim art with respect to their disclosures or affective aims. Arahmaiani is a contemporary Javanese performance artist, committed to Islam (her father's religion) but also engaged by Hindu–Buddhist beliefs (her mother's faith). She aims to shock and critique the sensibilities of Muslim viewers and participants. In her performance of "Breaking Words," she wrote *Allah* on white ceramic plates in Arabic. She invited audience members to write on them as well, and then smashed them against the wall.

The intent of this iconoclastic gesture was to shake participants loose from attachments that, in Arahmaiani's view, border on the obsessive-compulsive, not just to know Allah and to obey Allah, but to presume to act as Allah's sole custodian. For at least several viewers, the smashing of the plates was a humiliating, hurtful, even hateful blow to Allah and to their affective attachments to Allah. Complaints were lodged with the police at the opening performance, and also in subsequent forums where the artist appeared.

But her audacity is yet another tangent of an ICS at work beneath the gaze of most observers and beyond the logic of most analysts. Consider the moral status of this artist and her work. "If some artists aim at ethical pleasure through their work," notes George, the same scholar who has also written about Pirous, "perhaps we may say that Arahmaiani's strives for ethical hurt (not harm) or, better ethical unease. Arahmaiani is an artist of conscience, yet different people are made happy by different things [and so] object choices are not equivalent."[12] Arahmaiani seeks to raise the serious but tangled

Figure 5.1 Dashing the Allah plate.

question: in what context, and with what memories, does one appeal to happiness? In shattering the Allah plates, she hopes to trigger in others awareness of the history of injustice, a gesture toward recovering "happiness" or the collective good (*maslaha*) by reimagining what else may count as the good life other than "mere" worship of an object such as the Allah plate. In order to find alternative models of the good, one must first "touch" what is assumed to be the ultimate source of good and bad, hope and despair: the name Allah. Arahmaiani is even prepared to kill some forms of joy that her viewers take for granted when they see the name Allah. Yet she recognizes her own risk at having to live with the consequent unhappiness of others whom she has provoked.

A major part of the outcry against Arahmaiani was not just in relation to her "harm" or "offense" to Allah, but also her resort to visual art and performance as the means of communicating her message. Using Arabic as a pictorial rather than verbal sign is itself an Indonesian reflex that has parallels in the work of other artists, such as Abdul Djalil Pirous, discussed above, yet his is a visual not a performative wrestling with the tension between divine language and human aspiration.[13]

And so, the radical plurality of culture in the Muslim world not only has a long history in the sphere of Islamicate/Persianate empires, but it also has its expression in the quotidian practices of amulet making in Mayotte or Arabic orthography as art in Bandar Aceh or Jakarta for modern-day Indonesians. There is no one way direction that dominates; instead there are multiple local, national, transregional, and global publics that attend to the boundaries between religion and culture, never achieving consensus about their tastes but always seeking to influence others, to tip toward their perspective, and their interests, an ever-shifting balance between sacred/profane, religious/secular, acceptable/objectionable uses of art as at once a visual and a verbal metonym for the collective good. *Barzakh* logic beckons us to see religion and culture as always interactive, inchoate, and pervasive in the minds and hearts, the pens and persons of believers, whether Muslim, non-Muslim, secular, or agnostic. While no actor, agency, or outlook prevails, multiplying offshoots recur. The ICS, like its multiple sources, always has new faces and fresh visions.

Sometimes these visions become evident through more narrowly linguistic markers of ICS in Southeast Asia. It is often the case that Persianate influences are detected across the vast Indian

Ocean, but often they are masked as Iranian imports. Sometimes, even within a single volume the two registers—Persian as solely Iranian, and Persian as a larger cultural force, at once linguistic and multinational. Looking at Persian Sufis and musicians who traveled to Nusantara, an indigenous geographical marker for the Malay archipelago, as early as the 14th century, a Singaporean ethnomusicologist notes how common yet mistaken it is think that "Farsi speaking Sufi Indians from the Indian Sub-Continent are 'Persians from Iran', as mentioned in both early western sources and also in primary texts written by Malay scholars."[14] Yet the very next chapter in the same edited volume where one finds doubt cast on the solo Iranian identity of all Persian-speaking Muslims in Nusantara, the author upholds *all* Persian scholars as also Iranian. The title of his article signals the anachronistic, and distorted, national agenda of the evidence and arguments that follow: "The Role and Contribution of Iranian Scholars to the Islamic Intellectual Tradition in Indonesia from the Past to the Present."[15] It is impossible to erase such intellectual colonizing of the past in the service of present actors and interests, but one must cringe when a scholar declaims that "the Islamic Republic of Iran has been, and must be, a model for the Islamic world and any humanity-loving country across the world."[16]

In the face of both underreported migrations, and exaggerated retellings of the Persian past as an Iran-only endeavor, one must recuperate the multilayered, transnational trajectory of Persian as a Persianate trace beyond Iran. Just as Srinivas Aravamudan defined Islamicate as "the hybrid trace rather than pure presence or absence of Islam," so Persianate can be understood as the hybrid trace of Persian rather than its pure presence or absence as a *national* language.[17]

More realistic and more promising is an approach to Nusantara, past and present, as an enormous seascape in which one finds Persianate, and not just Persian or standalone Iranian-Persian, influences. If one thinks of India as a Persian cosmopolis embodying Persianate traces, as Richard Eaton has nimbly done,[18] one might also consider the florescence of a Persian cosmopolis in the eastern section of the

Indian Ocean, sometimes known as "the lands below the winds." Reflecting this geographical expanse of Persianate and the Persian cosmopolis, the Czech linguist Tomáš Petrů has authored an essay with this suggestive title: "'Lands below the Winds' as Part of the Persian Cosmopolis: An Inquiry into Linguistic and Cultural Borrowings from Persianate Societies in the Malay World.[19] His work can be helpfully coupled with the monograph from a British maritime historian, now teaching in Canada, Sebastian Prange: *Monsoon Islam: Faith and Trade on the Medieval Malabar Coast.*

Petrů's analysis is schematic, making only bullet points, not full-blown arguments, yet it opens up an array of new perspectives that do not deny the influence of Arabic but rather expand the frequent and imaginative dalliance between Persian and Malay abetted by commerce, religion, and an ethos of *adab* or civility. In brief, the historical canvas stresses the long middle period.

The period between the 13th and 17th centuries was the era of the most intense religio-cultural and linguistic exchange between the Persian *cosmopolis* and the Malay-Indonesian world. It was Muslim trade and its extensive networks which provided the major platform for transmission. The sources of this cultural transmission may be explained as two-fold: a) via the activities of Iranian merchants and sailors from Persia itself; b) by seamen, traders, diplomats, healers and other influential figures from Persianate sultanates or kingdoms of the Indian subcontinent, such as the Delhi sultanate, Gujarat, the Bahmanid Sultanate, or Golconda. These areas were exposed to several waves of Islamization, but the most important in relation to Southeast Asia was the third one, which took place during the period between the 11th and 14th centuries. This period witnessed increased missionary activity of the "Sufi saints," who played an instrumental role in shaping the Indo-Muslim culture of today's Pakistan, Bangladesh and large parts of India. And, as a result of the prevalently Sufi character of Perso-Indian sultanates and their representatives operating in the Indian Ocean trading network, the more tolerant, eclectic and mystically oriented *tasawwuf* (Sufism) became one of the key factors behind the Islamization of previously Hindu-Buddhist Maritime Southeast Asia. Intertwined with this discourse, other Persianate cultural elements followed suit, flowing to the areas east of the Bay of Bengal.

While the word "*adab*" is never used in the above analysis, the intertwined role of merchants and Sufis as the major actors in dispersing "Persianate cultural elements" across the Indian Ocean suggests that the Persianate ethos of hierarchical claims embodying reciprocity prevailed. While "tolerant and eclectic" projected good will and compassion for others, both were conveyed through a structured society where "trust" related to an Indo-Muslim, Persianate disposition to build networks across water as well as across land.

Focusing on Persianate influences cannot, and should not, obscure the openness that Persianate/Islamicate elements extend to other cultural elements, and it is "*adab*" that serves as the key term for looking at this larger trajectory of a Persianate ethos. Persianate, from the 7th century on, represents a bridge between Muslim/non-Muslim, elite/nonelite, center/periphery exemplars of an ICS. It also spurred generations of scholarly activity, from the literary and philosophical to the medical and physical sciences. And so Persianate is not merely a linguistic or territorial marker; it is also much more, a metaphor for global influences that derive from a networked society always in search of new potentials, a license to (re)create and to perpetuate an ICS based on *adab*.

The recent monograph of Sebastian Prange supports such a broad-scale analysis of the Persianate substrate of an Islamicate civilizational process. *Monsoon Islam* depicts not one but several networks at play. From a maritime oceanic rather than a territorial continental perspective, Prange sees multiple crisscrossing networks. "The role of Indian Ocean networks in the formation of a variegated but interconnected Islamic world in Asia," he argues, "underwrites the concept of Monsoon Islam... Neither a dichotomy of essentialized geographies—the harsh and forbidding desert versus the fluid and encompassing ocean—nor a simple binary between orthodoxy and diversity, Monsoon Islam is intended to capture the institutional and practical consequences of the interaction of Islamic beliefs and norms with other beliefs and norms in the absence of an Islamic political or social order. Out of this type of interaction emerged over time a different and distinct historical trajectory of Islam, one that contrasts with the historical experiences of Arabia, Persia, and North India but that was commonplace all across the medieval trading world of the Indian Ocean: an Islam that was shaped by the priorities and preferences of ordinary Muslim merchants as they traded and settled along the coastlines of monsoon Asia."[20]

In short, while Prange does not use either Islamicate or Persianate as key terms, his own key term, Monsoon Islam, provides yet another test case for the ICS, radiating out from Muslim mercantile networks but not limited either to Muslims as agents or Islam as religious practice in their everyday expression. Indeed, as Prange makes clear in his wide-ranging arguments, as also in his conclusion, it is Monsoon Muslims who must be engaged and rethought if we are to understand Monsoon Islam: "Monsoon Islam has eluded the attention of scholars in part because it is not so much about Islam as it is about Muslims: it is the history of how people, above all ordinary traders, used and reshaped Islamic precepts to address the specific challenges, opportunities, and settings they found themselves confronted by in their pursuit of profits."[21]

While Prange does survey the problems of reformist movements, and the dynamics between global and local forces, his range of evidence touches lightly on the modern period. Yet the modern period has imposed limits and new directions on Monsoon Islam and the range of Indian Ocean Islamicate options. Here as elsewhere the ICS must face limits when confronting the apparatus and the agents, the ideology and the power, of the nation-state. Those limits become evident in a new book on Muslim cosmopolitanism in the lands below the winds. A Singaporean Muslim academic, Khairudin Aljunied, affirms that a cosmopolitan trajectory does exist with Muslim overtones and undertones, and it can be found in places and persons identified with Islam, especially but not solely in Southeast Asia. There it becomes part of what the author labels, following Azyumardi Azra, Islam Nusantara.[22]

Khairudin correctly notes that "as a concept, Muslim cosmopolitanism suffers from being used too loosely and too indiscriminately to describe anything that Muslims say and do which points towards some degree of inclusivity." He looks to forms of everyday expression—"a style of thought, a habit of seeing the world, and a way of living"—all linked to Islam in its broadest formulation as *maqasid al-shariah*. *Maqasid al-shariah* means the purposes of Islamic law, specifically as they are defined in five mandates that apply to Muslims but also to all humankind: to preserve self, to preserve mind, to propagate via marriage, to preserve society, including property, and also, crucially, to preserve and defend belief in God.[23]

And who are the Muslim cosmopolitans of Southeast Asia? Among the many candidates Khairudin focuses on three prominent public intellectuals: Chandra Muzaffar, Azra Azyumardi, and also Hussin Matlib. Of these individuals, Azyumardi stands out because he, like Aljunied, is intent on demonstrating how Islam Nusantara, or Southeast Asian Islam, becomes a bridge to understanding Muslim cosmopolitan both regionally and globally. What distinguishes this approach is its historical focus and its contemporary expression. Surveying the advent of Islam to the archipelago, Azyumardi argues that while Malays, the dominant group, accepted Islam, they did not share features favored by its Arab-Persian predecessors and co-religionists. Theirs was an alternative Islam, one that, above all, accented accommodation with non-Muslims not merely as a necessity but also as a virtue. In other words, a sense of civility, identified by Hodgson and Salvatore as *adab*, pervaded their everyday outlook as also their public conduct.

Adab is especially crucial when engaging, and valuing, non-Muslims, but it is haunted by the shadow of *Islam politik* (political Islam). Khairudin follows Azyumardi in seeing it as an external challenge to the true core of tolerant or inclusive Islam, not least because Muslim cosmopolitans "have benefited much from the agency of non-Muslims in their midst, to withstand the intolerance of radical and extremist groups in Muslim Southeast Asia."[24]

Not just fringe or radical groups but also nation-states, their supporters, and their officials, are opposed to cosmopolitan ideals and practices. "That these states [Malaysia, Singapore and Indonesia] have yet to become responsible cosmopolitan states is unsurprising given that the very notion of cosmopolitanism runs contrary to what most states stand for. States often seek to impose a sense of allegiance and loyalty that would glue society together to achieve the state's ends."[25]

One must pause and stress that this blockage within the nation-state system exists not just in Southeast Asia but also in the rest of Asia and Africa as well as Europe and North America. It is subtle in expression and durable in its force. How do the state and its advocates restrict the contour, and so limit the influence, of cosmopolitanism? Let me provide some reflection on how its bright vision continues to be contested by both state and nonstate actors, within and beyond Islam Nusantara.

An example of the difficulty cosmopolitans face, even within the expansive frame of Islam Nusantara, has been illustrated by Jowel Canuday, a Filipino anthropologist.[26] He titled his brilliant Oxford DPhil dissertation: "Music, Dances, and Videos: Identity Making and the Cosmopolitan Imagination in the Southern Philippines" (2013). Canuday foregrounds his own approach in bold terms. He relies on fellow anthropologist Richard Werbner to document the importance of "others." "In modern Botswana, Werbner appropriates the notion of rooted cosmopolitanism in analyzing the characteristics of leading public intellectuals, crusaders for social justice, and valiant nationalist revolutionaries who are proud and assertive of their ethnic or other origins and home identities while recognizing the cultural good of being engaged with a variety of others."[27]

While these assessments effectively enrich our idea of a rooted sense of cosmopolitanism, they also raise the question: should rooted cosmopolitan agents be public intellectuals? Should their acts be defined by public and political activism? Can an ordinary person committed to peace and justice at home be regarded as rooted cosmopolitans? For Canuday rooted cosmopolitanism must be rooted not in the public square but at the level of the everyday and the quotidian. On such a level, particularly in Zamboanga and Sulu, Muslim majority islands of the Philippines, we see a broad range of actors who do not necessarily lead or actively participate in patriotic movements but just the same shape and share an imagined community that simultaneously celebrate home identity and relations with the other. Furthermore, we see at this level, marginalized agents taking active roles in the making of the cosmopolitan imagination with tools, modes, and relations of creative production, which can be regarded as improvisational. The fluid, indeterminate flow of everyday and quotidian life can provide us a lens in viewing a process of identity construction that does not stray from the cosmopolitan vision of ethical engagement of self and other even as its agents respond to unequal power relations and issues of social justice in their midst.

Inevitably, the techniques of this improvisation entangled Canuday in the vagaries of working indeterminately with local agents at the helm of VCD productions as he myself performed "the cosmopolitan engagement of fieldwork"; that is, he tried to highlight the relational dimension of improvisation that music video makers had cultivated with him in the same way that they would engage their collaborators in the improvisational process of VCD productions. Relevantly, his engagement points to his own attempt at improvising in fieldwork, seeing fieldwork itself as an improvisational practice, as had Llisa Malki.[28]

And so, there is always a fuzzy or *barzakh* logic at work, acknowledging artistic structures and practices but also relating them to broad political issues that are "outside" the sphere of culture, and yet influencing artists' vision of their collective future. "On the one hand," notes Canuday, "an armed secessionist movement seeks to consolidate and transform multilingual areas of Mindanao where Muslims are majority into a *Bangsamoro* (Moro nation) body politic that associates with the global Islamic ecumene. On the other, the Philippine state has pursued a sustained but fumbling effort of integrating Muslim Mindanao communities into its vision of a broader multicultural, multi-faith, and multi-linguistic Filipino nation that aligns with the non-secular democratic world."

A closer scrutiny of these contrasting nationalist imaginations, however, reveals a remarkable parallel between them. The two sides pursue homologous sentiments of nationalism that are far from ethnocentric but more reflective of the cosmopolitan sensibility of coming to terms within internal differences, both defined as "national." Both the Philippine state and Moro rebels project competing nationalist imaginations that offer a contrasting sense of rooted cosmopolitanism and of being cosmopolitan patriots who are also global citizens. Each adversary envisions a collectivity of multilingual and multicultural communities that is mindful of their variegated roots and desire for trans-local connections.

And it is just this clash of similar dispositions that leads to the following donnybrook, aptly etched by Canuday. "The state's and the rebels' cosmopolitan notions of the nation stopped right at each other's visions, ending where each other's imagined nation begins. These positions illustrate that when similar ideals of rooted cosmopolitanism actually exist on the same competitive political field, they complicate the notion of cosmopolitan nations and the case for patriotic cosmopolitans."[29]

What the above analysis from Canuday illustrates is the institutional limits imposed on Islam Nusantara owing to the preeminence of the state at molding discourse and promoting its vision of the imagined community in language that echoes, even as it overshadows, its rivals. If there is a pseudo-cosmopolitan spirit at work in the shadows of multiple regional entities, the Filipino state is a prime candidate proving its existence, as also its durability.

The same dilemma marks efforts to identify, then pursue Muslim cosmopolitanism beyond Islam Nusantara. A site where many have sought to locate, define, and defend cosmopolitan resources, actors, and projects is Iran. Keen insight into the slippery slope for a cosmopolitan agenda in 21st-century Iran comes from a volume edited by literary scholar, Lucian Stone.[30] Titled *Iranian Identity and Cosmopolitanism: Spheres of Belonging*, this edited volume explores the national and transnational sphere of Iranian sovereignty. Like Aljunied, Stone is alert to the grounding value of place, in his case, Iranian space. But is that space solely marked at home in Iran, or is it also diffused abroad through Iranians in exile? Successive authors in the Stone volume acknowledge the locational distance between themselves, Iranians abroad, and their "fellow protestors," Iranians at home. The former have the freedom to express, but no effective vocabulary; the latter have the experience of dissent, but no channel to voice it.

This difficulty is best framed in the tension between the two polar dispositions often cited above: belonging and longing. All who identify as Iranian claim a past that embraces nearly three millennia. Their historical vision is even longer than Islam Nusantara. It was Persians who challenged Greeks, conquered most of the Mediterranean world, endured the Arab conquest, and then created an Iranian epic, the *Shahnameh*, as well as Iranian Shiʻism. They forged a series of empires that endured until the modern period of first European, then American global hegemony. It is traces of that past that shape the options for the ICS with an Iranian accent. It proclaims Persianate as not just a national treasure but also a global resource. Yet the flexibility and subtlety of Iranian engagement with multiple registers of belonging (to some vision of the past) and longing (for some process of moral–political inclusiveness) is forever at risk of being collapsed into its opposite. As one contributor to the Stone volume, Farhang Erfani, observes, belonging and longing must converge, reinforcing one another, if cosmopolis is not to become a "fantasy of integration," allowing capitalist and metropolitan, rather than ethical and cosmopolitan, interests to prevail.[31]

And so in Iran as in Mindanao, as also in Singapore, Malaysia, and Indonesia, the flip side of genuine cosmopolitanism is a simulacrum: cosmopolitan in name, it claims authenticity yet subverts the reality of what is required for longing and belonging, or *maqasid al-shariah*, the genuine goals of a fully humane and universally inclusive Muslim society. Aljunied remains optimistic about a pervasive, enduring cosmopolitanism in Islam Nusantara. He offers several examples. There are cosmopolitan mosques with no restriction on women's attendance. There are Muslim bloggers who defy state strictures, and as nimble netizens, promote online ethics of tolerance, respect, and constructive criticism. There is also the artful use of women's head-dress, producing what could be, and is, labeled: "*hijabi*s as purveyors of Muslim cosmopolitanism." While all these sites of activity and portals of hope underscore the persistent cosmopolitan ethos of Southeast Asia, will it survive? Will it not only survive but prevail against the political headwinds that challenge and curtail its force? It is too early to tell but the forces of hope exist outside not within the state, in the bravado of artists as also the defiant intellectuals who are at once writers and activists. These are the truly heroic patriots, exemplars without flags or guns but restive for an ethos that expands, not reduces, their common humanity.

High on this roll call of exemplars without flags or guns is Alber Husin, to whom *Islamicate Cosmopolitan Spirit* is dedicated. Alber Husin was invaluable as a resource for both Jowel Canuday and me. We were shocked when Alber was killed in February 2013 at age 36. He was killed not by extremists but likely by a policeman, perhaps because he was an outspoken, and fearless, peace activist. Alber's passion for nonviolence inspired others in the Sulu community, and he remains the exemplar of "a gun-less warrior," an Islamicate advocate of cosmopolitan longing for an end to armed conflict and the dawn of lasting peace. This manifesto, fittingly, is dedicated to Alber Husin and his legacy.

Notes

1 Shahab Ahmed, *What is Islam?: The Importance of Being Islamic* (Princeton, NJ: Princeton University Press, 2015): 173.

2 *Sahih Bukhari* Volume 006, Book 060, Hadith Number 420. Cited online at: http://www.hadithcollection.com/sahihbukhari/sahih-bukhari-book-60-prophetic-commentary-on-the-quran-tafseer-of-the-prophet-pbuh/sahih-bukhari-volume-006-book-060-hadith-number-420.html (accessed May 30, 2020).

3　Franz Rosenthal, tr., *The Muqaddimah: An Introduction to History*, abridged and edited by N.J. Dawood (Princeton, NJ: Princeton University Press, 1967/2005): 430. Turki al-Faisal, the noted Saudi statesman and public intellectual, crafted a popular essay on the depth of Persian engagement with scientific skills quoting this same Tradition: "There is a tradition that states that the Prophet Mohammed (PBUH) once gestured toward his Persian companion Salman and said: 'Even if faith were near the Pleiades, men from among the Persians would attain it.'" *Tahrir Forum* (October 11, 2015). https://www.thecairoreview.com/tahrir-forum/ beauty-of-the-pleiades (accessed May 30, 2020). The word "*iman*" signifying faith, also extended to scholarship, reinforcing the notion that religion and culture were interwoven, not least in a Persianate template of science.

4　Sheldon Pollock has a variant approach to explaining the importance of "classical" languages in the formation and expansion of "cosmopolis" as a transnational network. According to Pollock, as quoted by Tomáš Petrů, "the 'foreign' language, in this case Persian, garners a great deal of influence, not as a vernacular, but as a medium that embodies a set of sophisticated concepts—more sophisticated than the local ones so that they stipulate imitation of their style and way of being across geographically vast areas." Yet the element that exceptionalizes Persian, and leads to the expansion of Persianate influence, is not its inherent superiority as a more sophisticated language, stipulating "imitation of style and a way of being," so much as a notion of accommodation and trust within hierarchy, to wit, *adab* conjoined with a process of *taskhir* or reciprocity that works across social, cultural, and linguistic boundaries.

5　Armando Salvatore, *The Sociology of Islam: Knowledge, Power and Civility* (Oxford: Wiley-Blackwell, 2016): 280.

6　One must also add that his writing style did not invite casual, bedtime reading. A scholar's scholar, he was densely referential in many passages of *The Venture of Islam*. The labor it takes to understand him is worth the effort, but it must be a continuous effort, as even his admirers have noted. Clifford Geertz, who wrote the longest and perhaps the most insightful review of *The Venture of Islam*, noted: "Hodgson's theme is the interaction of the Islamic and the Islamicate within Islamdom (the part of the world 'where Muslims and their faith are recognized as prevalent and socially dominant') across the centuries, and the shapes of conscience which that interaction has created. It is a theme he sustains clearly, and continuously, through fifteen hundred pages of the most intricate descriptive argument." And for Geertz, what results is "a magnificent achievement: a clear, comprehensive, beautifully researched, and, above all, profoundly felt account of a great spiritual tradition, a monument both to the faith of Muslims and to his own" (Clifford Geertz, "The Mysteries of Islam," *New York Review of Books* (December 11, 1975), 18–23).

7   Michael Lambek, "Certain Knowledge, Contestable Authority: Power and Practice on the Islamic Periphery," *American Ethnologist* 17(1) (February, 1990), 23–40. I have omitted some of Lambek's references in order to highlight the central point: texts take on variant meanings by contextual actors; even those that would be deemed problematic or "heretical" have local sanction due to inchoate or culturally valued practice. Many more such instances of magical "authority" are also cited and analyzed in the Persianate realm by Melvin-Koushi and Pickett.

8   Kenneth M. George, "Ethics, Iconoclasm, and Qur'anic Art in Indonesia," *Cultural Anthropology* 24(4) (2009), 589–621, also discussed in *Cultural Anthropology: Curated Collection 19—Everyday Islam*, edited by Kathryn Zyskowski (2014). see http://www.culanth.org/curated_collections/19-everyday-islam (accessed February 26, 2021).

9   Aziz al-Azmeh, *Islams and Modernities* (London and New York, NY: Verso, 1993): 60.

10 Charles Hirschkind, *The Ethical Soundscape: Cassette Sermons and Islamic Counterpublics* (New York, NY: Columbia University Press, 2006): 76. A more recent elaboration of how a Quranically attuned bodysoul functions can be found in Talal Asad, "Thinking about Religion through Wittgenstein," forthcoming in *Critical Times* (December 2020), to which I also have penned a response "Writing in the Eye of the Storm," detailing how *barzakh* logic helps us think more clearly about the sentient and emotive force of bodysoul imagery.

11 Kenneth M. George, *Picturing Islam: Art and Ethics in a Muslim Lifeworld* (Chichester, England: Wiley-Blackwell, 2010): 1–13. The entire monograph is much more than ethnographic art history

focused on individual Achinese/Indonesian artists. It makes a critical intervention into the debate about Islam—Islamic norms, values, practices, institutions—highlighting the role of the individual as a conscious subject of her/his own destiny through and with representational art that is both religious and much more: Islamicate, cosmopolitan, and enlivened by the spiritual pursuit of a higher good, in short, ICS, of which Pirous is a striking exemplar. An alternate vision of lifeworlds is provided in Mohammed A. Bamyeh, *Lifeworlds of Islam: The Pragmatics of a Religion* (New York, NY: Oxford University Press, 2019). Bamyeh offers a refreshing phenomenological engagement with Muslim lifeworlds as "the true social laboratories of invention" (p. 5) and while there is much to applaud in his juxtaposition and replacement of systems with lifeworlds as a key word of analysis, he does not address the multiple localities of Islam till the end: in his final chapter depicting Islam as global order (chapter 3), he begins to examine Islamicate empires and trade routes de novo, with no historical or etymological background (pp. 178–179), leaving the reader to wonder why this neologism suddenly applies to the Muslim world.

12 For further references, see Kenneth M. George, "Ethics, Iconoclasm, and Qur'anic Art in Indonesia," *Cultural Anthropology* 24(4) (2009): 589–621. There are also numerous YouTube sites featuring her work, e.g. https://do250.com/events/2019/3/17/arahmaiani-breaking-words (accessed May 30, 2020).

13 There are also numerous instances of Pakistani, Indian, and Iranian women artists who test the limits of self-censorship in artist work and/or performance art. Among them is the University of California (Berkeley)-educated Shirin Neshat. Neshat has mounted several exhibits of her photography, including the series *Women of Allah*, shown during the 1990s at major museums across the United States. For more on Neshat and other radical Islamicate feminists, see Bruce B. Lawrence, *Who Is Allah?* (Chapel Hill, NC: University of North Carolina Press, 2015): conclusion, 163–166. Like Neshat, these women artists may be attracted to utopian projects, on the edge of Muslim self-expression, but that imaginative leap qualifies them, like Neshat, as Islamicate cosmopolitan seekers, emboldened by *adab* not dwarfed by orthodoxy.

14 Hilarian Larry Francis, "The Persian and Arabian Musical and Cultural Impact on the Early Global Trade-Routes to *Lautan Melayu* (The Malay Sea)" in Syed Farid Alatas and Abdolreza Alami, eds., *The Civilisational and Cultural Heritage of Iran and the Malay World: A Cultural Discourse*, jointly published by Gerakbudaya Enterprise, Selangor, Malaysia and Cultural Centre, Embassy of the Islamic Republic of Iran, Kuala Lumpur (2018): 15–38. I am grateful to Professor Sajjad Rizvi (University of Exeter) for this reference as also for the book in which it is located.

15 Husain Heriyanto in Farid Alatas and Alami (2018): 39–57. There is, of course, another anachronistic assumption, to wit, that "Iranian Sufi teachers" in Nusantara were also Indonesian. Like Malaysia, Singapore, and also the Philippines, Indonesia only became a nation-state, albeit with permeable borders and multiple languages as well as ethnicities, in the mid-20th century.

16 Husain Heriyanto in Farid Alatas and Alami (2018): 56.

17 See Overview, n. 6, for a reference to this pioneering scholar and his elegant essay on Islamicate influences in 18th-century colonial literature from numerous sources.

18 See his recent monograph, Richard M. Eaton, *India in the Persianate Age 1000â€"1075* (London: Penguin Books, 2019).

19 Tomáš Petrů, "'Lands below the Winds' as Part of the Persian Cosmopolis: An Inquiry into Linguistic and Cultural Borrowings from Persianate societies in the Malay World," *Moussons* [Online], 27 (2016). https://doi.org/10.4000/moussons.3572.

20 Sebastian Prange, *Monsoon Islam: Faith and Trade on the Medieval Malabar Coast* (Cambridge: Cambridge University Press, 2017): 14.

21 Prange (2017): 318.

22 Khairudin Aljunied, *Muslim Cosmopolitanism: Southeast Asian Islam in Comparative Perspective* (Edinburgh: Edinburgh University Press, 2017): 86–91.

23 Aljunied (2017): xx.

24 Aljunied (2017): 170.

25 Aljunied (2017): 161.

26 I am indebted to the Carnegie Corporation of NYC for selecting me as a Carnegie Corporation Scholar of Islam in 2008, in order to pursue the study of minority citizenship in the Horn of Africa and

Southeast Asia. Both the earlier article on Ethiopia and now this engagement with Jowel Canuday, and his collaborator, Alber Husin, were made possible by the generosity of the Scholars Program, and I extend to its officers a long overdue, much deserved thanks for their confidence that one day I would link together the Muslim minorities of Ethiopia and the Philippines in a study that relates to the dilemma of national belonging and cosmopolitan longing.

27   Cited from Richard Werbner, "Reaching the Cosmopolitan Subject: Patriotism, Ethnicity and the Public Good in Botswana" in Pnina Werbner, *Anthropology and the New Cosmopolitanism: Rooted, Feminist and Vernacular Perspectives* (London: Bloomsbury, 2008): 175.

28   Allaine Cerwonka and Llisa H. Malki, *Improvising Theory: Process and Temporality in Ethnographic Fieldwork* (Chicago, IL: University of Chicago Press, 2007): 179. It is important to stress that "improvising theory" in fieldwork is fraught with personal danger not only to the ethnographer but also to her/his onsite facilitators. Alber Husin, a resource for both Jowel Canuday and me, was killed in February 2013. See Jowel Canuday's remarkable tribute to this fearless warrior for a world beyond war in *Mindanews*: https://www.mindanews.com/feature/2013/02/personal-essay-requiem-to-a-gun-less-warrior (accessed February 11, 2021). This manifesto is, fittingly, dedicated to Alber Husin and his legacy.

29   Jowel Canuday, "Music, Dances, and Videos: Identity Making and the Cosmopolitan Imagination in the Southern Philippines," Oxford DPhil Dissertation, submitted and approved 2013, ms., pp. 2–3. The preceding references, as also this direct citation, come from an unpublished version of the dissertation that the author kindly shared with me.

30   Lucian Stone is also an editor of the online book review provided by *Society for Contemporary Thought in the Islamicate World* (*SCTIW*).

31   Farhang Erfani, "Cosmopolitanism: Neither For, Nor Against, to the Contrary" in Lucian Stone, ed., I*ranian Identity and Cosmopolitanism: Spheres of Belonging* (London and New Delhi: Bloomsbury, 2014): 156. I am here summarizing an elaborate double-edged critique. Farhang Erfani, a specialist on Ricœur who teaches philosophy at American University, provides an extended meditation that is a brilliant satire on the conceits and dead ends of contemporary philosophy, but it

also conveys a heavy dose of self-criticism, leveled at the title of the volume "Iranian *Identity* and Cosmopolitanism." There is no single, monolithic *iraniyyat* (notion of Iranianness) either at home or abroad, he argues. While "the younger generation is thrilled by anyone advocating for Iranian–Americans," seeing the hyphen as "a cultural passport to being an official minority," Erfani locates himself "at the bottom edge of the previous disintegrated generation that is suspicious of the dash and considers it a cultural surrender. Not at home [in the US], this older generation has no hyphens, no center, and is suspicious of all messages" (p. 156). If there is a cosmopolis, he concludes, "the cosmopolis has a capital; it is Capital. As such it serves its metropolitan and not cosmopolitan interests" (p. 157).

6

Islamicate Cosmopolitan Spirit Beyond 2020

Islamicate Cosmopolitan Spirit (ICS) remains a living ideal with historical antecedents though it has no secure future beyond its several, mostly academic advocates. In my analysis I have made frequent mention of how uneven is the reference to Islamicate civilization—or to Islamdom or the Islamic ecumene—in some of scholarly assessments of the Afro-Eurasian ecumene, major zones marked by Islam. Such aporia have only increased during the modern period.

But now more than 40 years after Hodgson, we are witnessing an uptick in scholarly use of Islamicate. Though still restricted, recent publications augur the robust resilience of Islamicate as a qualifier for premodern cultural/intellectual engagement across creedal, sectarian, or linguistic borders in Afro-Eurasia. Most have appeared only in the past two decades, and many as recently as 2019–2020. All these publications can be reviewed as: academic journals, synthesizing studies, Persianate/Islamicate volumes, and edited books on the Persianate world, along with the prospect of new pedagogical and technological initiatives.

Before reviewing these indices of change toward an ICS at several portals of academic labor, let me cite two recent email exchanges that signal an ambiguous shift. Both exchanges came in February 2019,

Islamicate Cosmopolitan Spirit, First Edition. Bruce B. Lawrence.
© 2021 Bruce B. Lawrence. Published 2021 by John Wiley & Sons, Ltd.

the same month as I held the lunchtime seminar at the University of Exeter, with which I began this manifesto. One was from a Canadian philosopher, the other from a U.S.-based art historian. They veer in different directions.

The Canadian philosopher, Walter Young, is hopeful. Teaching at McGill's Institute of Islamic Studies, Young is motivated by the annals of philosophical disputation as a cross-cultural, multidisciplinary topic. At the University of Exeter, where I met him in February 2019, I asked him why he chose Islamicate as a descriptor in launching a new website, the SSIDD, or Society for the Study of Islamicate Dialectical Disputation, in 2016 (see https://ssidd.org). His reply:

> As far as my choosing "Islamicate," (rather than "Islamic" or "Arabic"), the answer is relatively simple. I am in this way, and several others, a Hodgsonian—not in a slavish fashion, or course, but in a "following the *ḥujja*" fashion. That is to say, especially when it comes to paradigms on the sweeping scale of world-historical phenomena (where I am—and always will be—much out of my depth), I go with what seem to me *the most rationally argued, comprehensive, and accurate models*—those with the greatest and most sensible explanatory power, requiring the least adjustment when they almost-fit-but-not-quite the more particular historical phenomena I may be studying. This latter condition is one reason why, for example, I love Hodgson but not Weber. Granted, "Islamicate" is more a descriptive term than a paradigm, but Hodgson provides a rationally argued definition that is wonderfully practical, to boot.

Even though the SSIDD website is recent, its user base limited, its broad appeal within the humanities is reflected, for instance, in the latest digital initiative, a new technological project focusing on making Persian, Arabic, and other Islamicate texts more readily available for scholarly use. Its acronym in tech language is: OpenITI AOCP, which stands for **Open I**slamicate **T**exts Initiative's **A**rabic-script **O**ptical **C**haracter Recognition Catalyst **P**roject. Funded by the Andrew Mellon Foundation in June 2019, its goal is to broaden the accessibility of Islamicate literary world to a new generation of scholars.

Recognizing that "the textual production of the diverse premodern Islamicate cultures stretching from modern Spain to South Asia is one of the most prolific in human history," still remains only partially available in the digital realm, the principal investigators of OpenITI AOCP "aim to establish a digital and organizational infrastructure … that will open up 'the great unread' of twelve hundred years of Persian and Arabic cultural production to rapidly proliferating and increasingly sophisticated 'distant reading' methods that until now have remained only partially usable in the study of Islamicate cultures." Theirs is the most ambitious initiative yet launched to expand the readership, and hence the influence, of Islamicate tangents within world history. Among its goals is "a comprehensive five-year plan for Islamicate corpus development and the improvement of Arabic-script OCR (including expansion into Urdu and Ottoman Turkish)." The project team includes an array of literary scholars and computer specialists from North America, the United Kingdom, and Western Europe, while their board of advisors boasts two leading Islamic studies scholars from the University of Maryland, Ahmet Karamustafa and Fatemeh Keshavarz, as also Intisar Rabb from Harvard Law School. Although the broad-scale impact of this project may not be felt for another decade, it bodes well for the global trajectory of Islamicate studies within and beyond the academy.[1]

While the future may unfold slowly but progressively toward a philosophical/juridical/historical window into Islamicate studies, the path forward in art history is less certain. My other Exeter email in spring 2019 was also exuberant. It came from Sugata Ray, an art historian at UC Berkeley. When I asked Ray to comment on his recent book, *Climate Change and the Art of Devotion: Geoaesthetics in the Land of Krishna, 1550–1850* (Seattle, WA: University of Washington Press, 2019), he replied:

> I engage with the Islamicate in my book on Braj (how can one not?!). Given the book's focus is on climate change, I argue that an eco-art history [i.e., an ecologically focused art history] of early modern South Asia brings together two discrete strands of

historiography: one centered on the political aesthetics of the Islamicate and the second engaged with ecological aesthetics. While the first chapter focuses on Mughal intersections in Braj, the last chapter focuses specifically on Islamicate cosmopolitanisms in Braj's temple architecture (via Lucknow and Rum). I have found the idea of the Islamicate to be productive and important, especially for complicating histories of Hindu art and architecture in the context of right-wing claims to an imagined authenticity.

Yet that goal—to use Islamicate "for complicating (essentialist) histories"—is less compelling for other art historians. Part of it is due to Ray's focus on South, Southeast Asia, and the Indian Ocean, not the geographic core of most reflection on Islamicate patterns or influence. Also, Ray himself is an innovator, broaching a new sub-field, eco-aesthetics, one that moves between and beyond charac-teristic disciplinary boundaries. One might even argue that there is a larger problem, to wit, that "Islamic" art history poses a problem still awaiting constructive scholarly engagement. Though Islamicate cosmopolitan taste pervades the Muslim networked zones in the Afro-Eurasian ecumene until the modern period,[2] art history as a topic to be explored, or a discipline to be enlisted, is largely absent from journals dedicated to the annals of Islamicate civilization, either premodern or modern.

Part of the problem is systemic: not only are humanities siloed from both social sciences and natural sciences in the 21st-century Euro-American academy, but art history is neglected or minimized in most other humanistic disciplines because it itself functions as a bridge discipline between visual, literary, and documentary studies, one requiring a deep local knowledge as well as broad critical skills. Too difficult to grasp in its breadth and its depth, it is reduced to a series of regional or specialized studies with a loose thematic con-nection to each other. Only a few bold, and also younger, practition-ers of art history, Sugata Ray among them, have begun to see the Islamicate turn as invaluable for their own scholarship across time and space. The great majority of art historians, whether directly or indirectly linked to civilizational studies, still stress the impossible vacuity of "Islamic art" while ignoring "Islamicate art" as a viable alternative. In an article originally published in 2012, the renowned Ottomanist Gülru Necipoğlu described how:[3]

> the emergence of the modern discipline of art history in nine-teenth-century Europe soon thereafter flourished in the Islamic lands. The absence of a totalizing concept of Islamic art before the modern era is therefore not a peculiarity of our own field. At least its invention is not more peculiar than the mirage of Western art, a category that was invented around the same time, along with its subordinate non-Western subfields. *The ambiguous appellation "Islamic Art" is indeed misleading, even though no satisfactory alternative has emerged* [emphasis added]. However, there seems to be a general consensus that the diverse and multifaceted visual cultures grouped under this problematic rubric do belong together in many ways. In this respect, Islamic art is not too different from Western art, an equally unwieldy subject with an unsatisfactory label that many have disowned without fashioning a better substitute.

What the defensive tone of this remark reveals is the difficulty of moving beyond regional comparisons—Western vs. Islamic—and also models of organizational and conceptual framing that are inherently weighted toward the West. This was exactly the problem that Hodgson faced over half a century ago: though *The Venture of Islam* was not published till 1974, by his death in 1968 he had addressed this same contradictory state of affairs. It is all the more surprising then that "Islamicate" or "Islamicate art" is absent from Necipoğlu's 2012 article, as also from the co-authored introduction she did to the 2017 two-volume *Companion to Islamic Art and Architecture* handbook that she co-edited with Finbarr Barry Flood, another major figure in premodern Islamicate art history. Once again, the comparison with Western art is broached, and both are deemed flawed as umbrella categories. The authors then announce a surprising new turn. "Despite its acknowledged problems," they assert, "no satisfactory alternative has emerged to replace the ambiguous appellation 'Islamic' art. 'Islamicate', a term coined by Marshall Hodgson in the 1970s [*sic*] to denote the adoption of cultural forms that originated in the Islamic world, independent of religious identities, *is gaining increasing acceptance* [emphasis added], especially among scholars concerned with the intercultural reception of artistic forms and practices that originated in the Islamic world."[4]

One would have expected examples illustrating how Islamicate has begun "gaining increasing acceptance." Yet the Flood/Necipoğlu volumes, while commendable for the scope and depth of their treatment of various stages and sites, exemplars and examples of Islamicate art production, do not explain or justify "the increasing acceptance of 'Islamicate,'" The co-editors cite but one case study: the 1996 essay by Phillip Wagoner, a South Asian art historian. They provide no further evidence of why and where and how "Islamicate" is "gaining increasing acceptance." A brief glance at Wagoner's essay, delivered as a conference paper more than 25 years ago,[5] explains why "Islamicate" has endured and still offers value to art historians. Here is the crux of Wagner's argument:

> An expanding Islamicate civilization, according to Hodgson, came closer than any other medieval society to establishing a common world order of social and even cultural standards. The acceptance of Islamic cultural norms could and did occur even in states which remained independent – like Vijayanagara and Norman Sicily – and were never subject to political domination by the caliphate or any of its successor states. The impact of this cultural hegemony was in the area of secular culture rather than of religion. What Hodgson speaks of are "standards of taste" or "social and cultural standards," and he pointedly characterizes these cultural phenomena not as Islamic, but as "Islamicate." Hodgson reserves the adjective "Islamic" to mean "of or pertaining to Islam" in the proper, the religious, sense; he coins the term "Islamicate" to refer more broadly to "the social and cultural complex historically associated with Islam and the Muslims, both among Muslims themselves and even when found among non-Muslims."[6]

Even with the recurrent debate—at once ongoing and endless—about how to distinguish "religious" from "cultural," Hodgson forged ahead with some clarifying language that resonates beyond art history but has not, till recently, captured the imagination of art historians.

The latest, and in some ways most sophisticated, effort to redeploy "Islamic" art beyond the conventional dichotomy, either stated or implied, of Western/Islamic art comes from an Ottomanist: Wendy M.K. Shaw. Her earlier monographs (2003/2011) explored museums and painting, while her articles, including one in the Flood/Necipoğlu volume (2017) discussed above, looks at the limits of implicit or explicit norms of value in reviewing, then evaluating the material production as well as the historical trajectory of "Islamic" art. Her most recent book, *What is "Islamic" Art?* deftly weaves together indigenous with exogenous sources of interpretation, bracketing Foucault with Ibn 'Arabi, Said with Ghazali etc. in 10 chapters that teem with insight but also challenge extant analyses of "Islamic" art.[7] Even while agreeing with her central observation—that the Western gaze lingers even in perspectivism—and her proposed correction—to move out of perspective, embracing "the decentered subjectivity of polyhedral isometric geometry"[8]—I would argue that it is not enough to propose multifocality as the alternative to a Euro-normative perspective. The dichotomy of Islamic/Western lingers; it also pervades her alternative use of "Islamic." At the outset Shaw mentions that analysis of Western art "might be better termed Christianate." She goes on to explain that Christianate "underscores the modern transposition of premises informed by *European Christianity as culture which permeate secular Western societies and which often serve as a measure for the assimilation of those designated as other* [emphasis added]."[9]

I italicize the crux of Shaw's argument because the concept of this scholarly precommitment to a religious culture within an allegedly secular society is traceable to Hodgson. In a footnote Shaw mentions "Marshall Hodgson's much debated term 'Islamicate'" but then avoids any further reference to Islamicate, citing instead Shahab Ahmed's labeling of this term as problematic, a labeling that is itself problematic as discussed above.[10] We are left with "Islamic" in inverted commas but with no alternative revisionist terminology. Islamicate begs for reconsideration.

Journals

Such reconsideration can be found in two recent journals. They have different foci—one contemporary, the other premodern—but both announce Islamicate in their titles. Recognizing the value of a virtual presence, both explore Islamicate approaches to intellectual history online. The oldest is barely a decade old: *The Society for Contemporary Thought and the Islamicate World* (*SCTIW*) was launched in 2010. Its website, SCTIW.org, boasts both a book review and debate forum. One of its editors, Lucien Stone, helped form an eclectic group with inclusive links to all periods and perspectives of world history. Though Islamicate is never defined, it is used as a moniker "to promote new directions in scholarship and creative activities related to the interface of so-called Eastern and Western movements." In other words, Islamicate serves more as an empty signifier than as an analytical key term. In one sense the stated purpose of the collective sounds hopelessly vague and aimlessly utopian: to define the Islamicate world as "embodying a kind of limitless zero-world, a vast territory of thought, experience, and imagination through which some of the most powerful currents circulate at will." Despite its conceptual limits, the review subset of *SCTIW* captures a wide array of topics on major books that have garnered reviews elsewhere but are reviewed here with cross-disciplinary and broad gauged verve, a desire to explore in-betweenness, the fuzzy or *barzakh* logic at play in all areas of modern knowledge.

Quite opposite in structure and purpose is *Intellectual History of the Islamicate World* (*IHIW*). Grounded in premodern history, it is available online but also in print. Since 2013 it has been published by Brill, under the editorship of German Islamicist Sabine Schmidtke, now at the Institute for Advanced Studies (IAS) at Princeton. Though temporally restricted to premodern subjects, issues, and publications, its declared purpose is at once transcultural, multicreedal, and interdisciplinary. It announces that: "In the medieval, late medieval and pre-modern world of Islam, Muslims, Jews and Christians constituted a unique cultural and intellectual commonality... The journal *Intellectual History of the Islamicate World* provides a forum for research that systematically crosses the boundaries between three major disciplines of academia and research, viz. Islamic Studies, Jewish Studies and the study of (Eastern) Christianity. It aims to promote a new understanding of intellectual history in all its facets throughout the Islamicate world, from its emergence until modern times and from different methodological perspectives."[11]

Though its editors never define Islamicate world, one must infer that Islamicate as a descriptor crosses boundaries, creedal as well as intellectual and geographic, since it connects two well-established fields, Islamic studies and Jewish studies to a trajectory that has yet to become a full-fledged field, at least in the Euro-American academy: the study of Eastern Christianity. In short, despite its definitional gaps, its editors aim to expand the notion of ICS, making it a foundational not peripheral element of the academy, promoting a new spirit of inquiry that boasts of *barzakh* logic throughout the premodern Islamicate world, also known as the Islamic ecumene or Islamdom.

Reference Books

Beyond journals, there need to be comprehensive studies that synthesize and integrate Islamicate/Persianate perspectives into world history. I had hoped to locate, then analyze a list of monographs and reference works utilizing while also expanding Hodgsonian categories, including Islamicate. Yet there exists in 2020 but a single, solitary effort to synthesize Hodgson into the larger ambit of world history. While both Huricihan Islamoğlu and Armando Salvatore have propelled Islamicate world history to the forefront of their own disciplinary analyses, it is Salvatore who has now expanded his Hodgsonian labor to include a monumental, broadly teleological handbook that takes up the challenge of tracing Islamicate civilization across several periods and in all parts of the known world or ecumene. Salvatore serves as senior editor for the most recent of the

Wiley-Blackwell reference works: with Roberto Tottoli and Babak Rahimi, Salvatore has produced *The Wiley-Blackwell History of Islam* (Chichester, England: Wiley-Blackwell, 2018) (hereafter the *WBHI*).

Because of its unique position in the reemergent field of Islamicate studies, the *WBHI* warrants close consideration. Over a decade in preparation, it includes an introduction, seven parts, and 28 chapters. It represents a masterful, extended reflection on Islam within the domain of world history, inspired by and loyal to Hodgson's vision. Though it also provides correctives to Hodgson, it accepts his challenge to forge a new periodization, in seven subsets:

1. Late Antique Beginnings (up to 661 CE)
2. High Caliphate (661–946)
3/4. Earlier, then Later Middle Periods (946–1453)
5. *Early Modernity* (1453–1683).

Followed by:

6. Rise of European Powers (1683–1882).

And then:

7. Colonial Subjection and Postcolonial Developments (1882 to present).

I italicize the Fifth Period or Part V because of its central importance for Islamicate usage. The benefit of this revisionist periodization is matched by novel rethinking of major elements in the tapestry of the Afro-Eurasian ecumene over almost 1,500 years. In its outline, as also in its contributions, it supports the notion that the high-water mark of Islamicate civilizational endeavor, and the emergence of an ICS, was not the medieval or even the late medieval but the early modern period. The full title for part V is: "Early Modernity *and* Civilizational Apogee (ca. 1453–1683)." The introductory preface to this part of a staggeringly diverse, wide-ranging reference work sets the tone for what follows:

Islamic history in this epoch unfolded within the broader global context which set the stage for the rise of the modern world. From the mid-15th to the late 17th centuries the globe saw a dramatic increase of connectivity across both the Old and the New Worlds. The Afro-Eurasian hemisphere underwent a qualitative change particularly across the Indian Ocean and on the new Atlantic routes. European overseas explorations were primarily responsible for this connectivity leap, with the colonization of the Americas, Africa, and parts of Asia—but so were Indian, Persian, and especially Ottoman travelers who ventured across the Indian Ocean pursuing economic and political gains. (p. 23)

In other words, Europe, formerly a frontier region, became the new hub of global connectivity. Yet Muslim power did not succumb to European hegemony. By the **late 17th** century the leading Muslim polities had asserted a distinctive type of Islamicate cosmopolitanism, nourished by sophisticated courtly and marketplace cultures, integrated social life, and centralized spiritual and administrative authorities. *In sum, Islam by 1683 had become truly Afro-Eurasian.*[12]

The pithy concluding sentence is italicized because it recapitulates a central argument of this manifesto: by the end of the 17th century *Islam—that is, Islamicate cosmopolitan civilization—had become truly Afro-Eurasian.* While it is impossible to elaborate on the content of all the chapters either in part V or in the volume as a whole, the above excerpt illustrates two crucial dimensions of Islamdom and Islamicate civilization. First, Islam was not linked to one area or one region, much less one language or defining culture. Second, the innovative and creative spirit of a piebald Islamdom did not die after the Middle Periods (946–1453) but actually peaked during the time of initial European expansion, including exploration of both the Americas and parts of the Afro-Asian hemisphere (1453–1683). The question remains: how did that influence of an Islamicate trajectory in world history fare after 1700? Did it integrate into the "modern" world, or did it remain as a substantial but bypassed outlier from the premodern era?

Persianate—Within or Beyond Islamicate?

To assess the influence of modernity, many scholars have opted to emphasize the distinctiveness of the Persianate in a broad trajectory of cultural influence, one that tends to assume the emergence of a modern nation-state as its inevitable outcome. At the same time, the Persianate is elevated, isolated, and stressed apart from the Islamicate, almost as if to concede that cultural influence is linguistic and linked to the "modern" secular state.

This double move—to accent the Persianate and separate it from the Islamicate—is evident in two edited volumes. Consider A.C.S. Peacock and D.G. Tor, eds., *Medieval Central Asia and the Persianate World: Iranian Tradition and Islamic Civilization*. This edited volume brings together a range of essays geographically and temporally circumscribed, focusing on Iran eastward and northward from the earliest to the later Middle Periods (750–1150). These essays project a distinct literary focus: to trace and elaborate "the emergence of New Persian as a literary and administrative language and an even more explicit regard for the pre-Islamic Iranian past, most famously signaled by the composition of the masterpiece of Iranian literature, Firdawsi's *Shahnama*." Yet that literary turn is complicit with, and complicated by Persianate dynasties that are ethnically Turkish, to wit, the Ghaznavids and the Seljuqs, and so the related purpose of this volume is to explore "the larger significance and cultural continuity of the Persianate dynastic period in the eastern Islamic world."[13]

Though never directly stated, the limit to this quasi-nationalist approach to Persianate longings and belongings emerges in the following volume, also edited by A.C.S. Peacock. Titled: *Islamisation: Comparative Perspectives from History*, it is much broader in scope than the preceding volume. Its goal is to understand what is meant by Islamization and how a cross-regional, interdisciplinary approach illumines its often competitive, and sometimes contradictory, features. It tries to answer queries on why the greatest centers of Muslim population exist outside the original sites of the Middle East, or Nile-to-Oxus region. Questions about the protracted connection between pre-Islamic language, culture and practices and the turn, or return to, what is defined as Islamic pervade many of the chapters, for instance chapter 11 on al-Andalus (Maribel Fierro) and chapter 12 on the Oromo in Ethiopia (Marco Demichelis, with other chapters on sub-Saharan Africa, the Balkans, Central Asia, South Asia, and also Southeast Asia and China). One astute reviewer has noted how: "several chapters critically explore dynamics of Islamization in relation to models of 'Arabisation' (Reuven Amitai, Maribel Fierro), 'Persianisation' (Blain Auer), Turkicisation (Peacock) and even 'Jawisation' (Philipp Bruckmayr), as frameworks for interpreting broader processes of social and cultural transformations across the broader regions of the Middle East, South, Southeast and Central Asia."[14]

What one misses here is the explicit distinction between Islamicization and Islamization, made earlier by Wagoner.[15] Each of the regional languages that facilitates Islamicate modes and values is better adduced as a cultural than a religious project "one inter-preting (but also facilitating) broader processes of social and cultural transformation" (p. 855). The expansive canvas is geographically compelling but still analytically understated. One would like to know how local culture and foreign agents, whether travelers or merchants, soldiers or Sufis, managed the conflicts, at once inevitable but also fluctuating, between Islam and competing nodes of allegiance. The cumulative evidence suggests that an Islamicate patina veils these competing forces, even while a cosmopolitan spirit lurks behind, beneath, and between them. The absence of framing language, and also Hodgsonian neologisms, limit the value of this volume, as also the previous volume. Revisionism requires a new vocabulary as well as fresh archival, textual, and ethnographic research.

Yet terminological revisionism—the search for more accurate, insightful key words[16]—is not sweeping world history, nor do historians share a transregional networked view of parity and reci-procity between major actors in world history, especially since the putative rise of the West from the 16th century onward. Islam may have been revalued but there persists an accent on the early period as both defining and exceeding all later developments. Even in the early period, specifically, the period identified as Late Antiquity, it is Islam *qua* religion and Arabic as canonical language that continue to be prized.

Ironically, however, the lack of attention to *Islamicate* elements in Late Antiquity is not matched in academic assessment of *Persianate*, at least in the most recent period. When we survey new monographs from other scholars, themselves engaged less by Late Antiquity than by the expanded Middle Periods, we find Persianate in the ascent. That ascent is worth charting, its explanation still elusive, its larger trajectory still in doubt.

There are two recent books that herald an expanded Persianate world, albeit with different emphases. Both were published in 2019, one from Brill, Abbas Amanat with Assef Ashraf, eds., *The Persianate World: A Shared Sphere*; the other from the University of California Press, Nile Green, ed., *The Persianate World: The Frontiers of a Eurasian Lingua Franca*. Both volumes expand the notion of Persianate beyond their predecessors, including the Tor/Peacock volume, which still posits an original Iranian ethos, in quasi-nationalist terms, to which other groups in variant ways respond.

By contrast, Abbas Amanat, with Assef Ashraf, *The Persianate World—Rethinking a Shared Sphere* announces, then explores "multiple pathways to the Persianate."[17] Most of these pathways are across Central Asia and South Asia, though the latter is accented. In effect, South Asia, broadly reconceived, exceeded the national borders that now demarcate Iran, Afghanistan, Pakistan, India, and Bangladesh as independent nation-states, each with their own historical parameters that also become boundaries, excluding as much as including elements from their collective past. In the essays themselves the temporal markings drive the geographical analyses. Consider the overview, and sequence, of chapters. Assef Ashraf's introductory essay maps the entire field of Persianate studies more thoroughly than any of its predecessors yet it ends with a mixed note about Persianate prospects, noting "a fascinating legacy that is only beginning to regain relevance in today's transnational and transregional approaches to history, literature, social studies and gender... Persianate studies can aim to reconnect seemingly disparate geographical disciplines by invoking a shared legacy" (p. 62).

Yet the essays that follow almost seem to belie the relevance of Persianate studies to the contemporary world order and its narrowly presentist priorities. The accent remains on "legacy" (from the past) rather than "relevance" (for the present) or "optimism" (for the future). The scourge of teleological "progress," always marked by inverted commas, limits the reach of Persianate influence. Eaton's essay, for instance, is temporally expansive, including two millennial periods—1,000 years for a Persian cosmopolis, another 1,000 years for its Sanskrit counterpart—the two cosmopolitan projects overlap and intertwine south of the Hindu Kush mountain range, namely, in southern Asia, known for centuries as simply Hindustan, to distinguish "India" from its neighbors, yet both end before the modern period. If the Sanskrit cosmopolis is eclipsed by the Persian cosmopolis for 500 years (1400–1900), it in turn is eclipsed by the British Empire, then incipient nationalisms, with no "modern" sequel.

Even more narrow temporally and geographically is Thibaut d'Hubert, exploring Persianate vernacular resources in the region of Bengal, that is, the Bay of Bengal, with vivid depiction of "marvels" from a 17th-century courtier/poet in present-day Myanmar. For Asfar Moin the Persianate is a vigorous medieval idiom, providing an aperture into multiple saints' complexes across present-day Central Asia and South Asia, with attention to how the bodies of royalty and their repositories gradually eclipsed those of saints, a process that culminated in 17th-century Mughal India. Waleed Ziad, in an essay adorned with maps and charts as well as figures, explores Sufi networks that crisscross Central and South Asia, focusing on a single order, the Naqshbandi-Mujaddidi, in the late 18th and 19th centuries. There is a single essay that focuses on a vital area adjacent to Central Asia, the Caucuses. It extends haltingly into the 20th century: Hirotake Maeda examines the religious–national identity of a Caucasus family, with Georgian–Armenian ties, reflecting a corner of the Persianate World from the 19th–20th century. It is a world closing down rather than opening up, and a similar deescalating teleology lies beneath the detailed tapestry of genealogical and spatial filiations that characterizes Joanna de Groot's forensic case study of a Baluch family (overlapping Afghanistan and Iran, as also part of Russian-controlled Central Asia).

But the most explicit reference to a drama conveying the march of time that highlights the *terminus ad quem* of a vibrant Persianate realm occurs in the final essay. It comes from the South Asian historian, Nile Green, the editor of the other *Persianate World* volume to appear in 2019. Green's is an exquisite, protracted argument against the notion of progress. Titled "The Antipodes of 'Progress': A Journey to the End of Indo-Persian," his chapter demonstrates that it was not just British colonial practice (to shift from Persian to English as the language of record for the East India Company) in the early 19th century (1837) but also the related movements, one indigenous (proclivity for Urdu and other regional languages), the other external (lack of technical vocabulary for modern machinery and industrial activities), that signaled the demise of Indo-Persian and so of Persianate culture in late colonial Hindustan. "Progress," defined by Europeans, seems to portend "the end of Indo-Persian," favored by Hindustani elites.

Since Green both lauds and limits Persianate influence throughout Eurasia, we should not be surprised that the same subtle but downward teleological thrust is present in the volume that he himself edits, a volume also titled: *The Persianate World*. Even though some of the authors, notably Eaton, Amanat, and Thibaut d'Hubert, overlap, the Green sequel volume contrasts with Amanat/Ashraf in its territorial reach. Yet in his timeframe, Green follows Eaton in underscoring the Persianate world/cosmopolis as millennial and premodern: only the opening date varies, Green suggesting that it covered slightly more than a millennium (ca. 800–1900), while for Eaton it was precisely 900–1900. The final period, ca. 1800–1920, is decisive: it traces multiple sites where Persianate culture is tested in new empires, as also in new nations, but always with mixed results that bode ill for Persianate options.

One would like to hope that the goal of both the Assef/Amanat and the Green volumes succeeds: to inspire the development of a new academic discipline titled Persianate studies. Let me revisit the evidence and the arguments. Ashraf announces his intent, shared with Amanat, at the outset of the volume: to cross national boundaries, in order to explore "culture-based" connections that show a transnational which is also post-national historical moment where Persianate studies finds a home but also contrasts with its adjacent fields, to wit, Islamic studies, Middle East studies, Central Asian studies, and South Asian studies.[18] Amanat later offers several interrelated arguments as to why Persianate studies can emerge as a new field of study, paralleling "the Middle East," which never existed as a term or object of academic study till after World War II.[19]

Yet it is Spooner's final essay in the Green volume that casts a pall, and renders a verdict, on all that preceded it:[20]

> The Persianate millennium finally ended in the way it had begun, as a result of severe social disruption… The competition between the British and the Russians, known as the Great Game, caused the final eclipse of the Persianate millennium, breaking up the ecumene into colonial territories that eventually became nation-states on the Western model. The socioeconomic dynamism that had created the paths for the spread of Islam and the Persian language had lost its driving force, and its cultural unity was divided by political boundaries. When the Islamic revolution in 1979 finally reshaped what had remained of Iran's premodern social structure under the final Pahlavi dynasty, the century-long half-life of the Persianate millennium was over, and the rate of social change accelerated.

Even if one challenges the implicit determinism of Spooner's analysis, it demonstrates two converging elements that shrink the status of Persianate options in the present-day academic world, as also popular understanding of a Persianate past. First was the 18th–19th century shift from a polycentric to a Eurocentric world history, limiting the cultural fluidity at the core of Persianate practice. The Chinese were outliers to the new world order, while the British and the Russians pursued strategic interests that denied Persianate options. All three groups augured what followed: the emergence of the nation-state, modern-day nationalism, carving up the ecumene into units focusing on a unified past, at once monolingual and ethno-preferential. One language, one group, one nation in one state became an unofficial motto, if not an explicit practice, throughout Afro-Eurasia, and while all minorities were put at risk, cultural practices that were polyvalent also declined or disappeared. Persianate became either challenged or obsolete in regions where it had succeeded, at the same time that Iranian nationalism derided Arabic or Turkish elements in its own history that precluded a limited Iranian–Persian national identity.[21]

Both these edited books help to chart the past of a Persianate world, but in the face of new obstacles to academia in general and area studies in particular, are they sufficient to spark a new academic discipline? Valuable as they are for historians, filling in missing characters, narratives, and activities of the Persianate world, these books also underscore still larger aporia, among them archival resources for telling the larger story of the Persianate ethos across time and place. If one looks merely at the history of Mughal India, one can find countless examples of Persianate literary culture that have been ignored, by local as also exogenous scholars. Consider the prominent 17th-century courtier for Shah Jahan, Chandra Bhan Brahman. Interest in Brahman is now revived, due to a lively biography by Rajeev Kinra. Apart from the argument about Brahman's legacy, however, there lies the neglect of the Indo-Persian literary production of the great Mughals. Major scholarship on the political, military, economic, and bureaucratic aspects of Mughal rule abounds,[22] yet the genre of literary labor that Chandar Bhan exemplifies—one linked to 17th/18th-century Indo-Persian *tazkiras*—has been routinely ignored. "This is not just a loss for Western scholarship," observes Kinra, since "many of these texts have faded into obscurity even in India … [at the same time that they] are often difficult to locate even in *Persian* printed editions."[23] And so what is needed for another generation of dedicated scholars, likely from beyond South Asia but focused on its larger role in world history, is an effort to explore the treasure trove of cultural production that led Mughal India, in Kinra's words, "to be viewed all over the wider Persianate world as a haven for intellectual freedom and literary genius."[24] More than a parochial matter for students of South Asia or the Indian Ocean, Kinra's ambition—to understand the Persianate world "as a haven for intellectual freedom and literary genius"—not only offers a necessary corrective to Orientalist or Western triumphalist views of the "decadent East" but also a window into how Persianate studies, rightly deployed, could be an anchor for comparative history.

It is that further step into a platform for comparative history that exceptionalizes the introduction to Green's edited volume. In his introduction, Green warns that we need to "de-provincialize the Persianate world from its familiarly Indo-Iranian moorings by making a more robust case for a 'world' that encompassed the greater part of the Eurasian continent." How to make this leap? "By bringing into the often narrowly Indo-Iranian historiographical conversation the work of scholars working on Persian texts that circulated as far apart as China, Siberia, Inner Asia, the Caucasus, the Volga-Urals and even some regions of the Indian Ocean." And it is perhaps for this reason that Green subtitles his volume: *The Frontiers of a Eurasian Lingua Franca*.

"Such a de-centering of Iran is deliberate, because to situate Iran at the perennial 'center' of a Persianate 'zone' or 'world'," argues Green "is not merely an expression of methodological nationalism. It is also a plain anachronism that negates the historicity of the Persianate world in all its capacity for dynamism, multiplicity and evolution."[25] And this ploy relates directly to cosmopolitan underpinnings. "If scholars now take for granted the notion that Persian was a shared lingua franca, it is important to identify more precisely who shared it, and for what (and indeed whose) purposes they did so. In focusing on the five centuries [1400–1900] that most densely marked both the making and unmaking of one of Eurasia's greatest lingua francas, *The Persianate World* is an exercise in tracing the contours and constraints of the cosmopolitan."[26]

110

But no less important are the exploration of geography and the testing of its limits. Here at last we find an analysis of how "Islam" and "Persian" intersect, enlivening both Islamicate and Persianate as qualifiers for the affective experience of Islamdom through Afro-Eurasia in the premodern period. "His [Hodgson's] Persianate model assumed two things: an Islamic (or at least culturally 'Islamicate') context in which Persian (and Islam) were in a position of cultural and political dominance; and, by extension, a geography confined to what used to be called the eastern Islamic world (or as Hodgson himself preferred, the 'Persian zone')."[27] In order to advance the vision of an ICS one cannot replace one particularism (nationalist) with another (Islamic). The difficult but necessary labor is to unhinge all bounded, and hinged, notions of identity, and to explore the transient yet transnational ethos of hope embodied by *adab*, the key term for both Persianate and Islamicate cosmopolitan longing.[28]

Two further elements from Green's introduction underscore the flexibility and appeal of the Persianate in Central and South Asia.

> Enabling the geographic expansion of the Persianate world's frontiers between around 1200 and 1500 were two key institutions that helped not only to disseminate the existing personnel of written New Persian (henceforth simply Persian), but also to produce new ones. It was these institutions of learning that would incrementally render Persian a learned second language rather than a written mother tongue. The Turkic ascendance of the eleventh and twelfth century was, in processual terms, more influential for its institutional than its bibliographical innovations. For by way of the *madrasa* and the *khanaqah*, the school and the convent, the Ghaznavids and particularly the Saljuqs patronized two new types of enduring institutions that not only enabled the production of more Persian texts but more importantly, reared new generations of producers and consumers of written Persian. Funded by property endowment (*waqf*), these new institutions for the overlapping parties of *'ulama* and Sufis expanded through the new territories that were conquered by the Ghaznavids in India and the Saljuqs in Anatolia.[29]

And equally important for the institutional growth of Persianate culture there emerged chanceries:

The subsequent rise of Persian-using chanceries in Lahore then Delhi and beyond, coupled with the immigration of "Turko-Persian" settlers, generated new spoken vernaculars that would in time develop written forms that were more hegemonically "Persianate," that is, graphically, lexically and generically Persianized. Most importantly, these included the various North Indian vernaculars generically referred to by medieval authors as Hindwi ("Hindi," that is, "Indian"). Compared to the older written literary traditions of Armenian and Georgian, which took Persian terms, tropes, and even genres but while remaining distinctive both orthographically and otherwise, these broadly Indic Turkic languages and their literatures were much more clearly "Persianate" in the dominant-partner sense that Hodgson intended.[30]

Beyond his own expertise and interest in Islamicate Asia, Green bends comparative world history in a new direction. He offers a further way of depicting the ICS, across Africa as well as Persianate Asia, a double frontier of linguistic, cultural, social, and moral expansion. It is a vision that meshes deftly with what another comparativist, Ronit Ricci, has called "the Arabic cosmopolis of South and Southeast Asia."[31] Whether or not these overlapping visions can be realized, its very expression, 50 years after the demise of Hodgson, is evidence of a smoldering hope for what Huricihan Islamoğlu calls "a world history worthy of the name."[32]

★★★★★★★★★★★

Each of the other tangents noted above focuses on publications related mostly to Persianate studies. There are: academic journals, reference tomes, topical volumes, and now the two newly edited books just discussed. Almost all these publications are dedicated to Persianate studies, with a side glance at Islamicate overlaps and parallels. But there also have been pedagogical shifts. They are still in flux, and because of the logistics involved, it often takes 4–5 years from a conference to the appearance of a volume of essays, as noted in the two recently published volumes of edited chapters both titled *The Persianate World.* Yet one must also note that their readership is limited: only a small percentage of world historians, those attune to hemispheric transformations, in micro as well as macro history, will read the resulting books. For this reason, it is important to note that primarily from Vienna and Chicago, with a side glance at Boston and New York, we can espy a new generation of scholars trained to think of Persianate/Islamicate networks as the foreword edge of a cosmopolitan agenda across Eurasia. The most recent major pedagogical workshop with this focus took place in Vienna, and it took place in June 2019. Online there appeared the announcement from Paolo Sartori, a leading Italian Persianate scholar, now a senior fellow at the Institute of Iranian Studies in the Austrian Academy of Sciences that he would spearhead a new initiative offering instruction on how to pursue cultural documentation in Persianate Eurasia (15th–19th centuries). The goal of this summer school was "to familiarize students with documentary and archival practices in the so-called Persianate world, i.e., a broad portion of Eurasia otherwise known as the Balkans-to-Bengal complex, with a linguistic focus on Persian and Turkic rather than Arabic, preparing students to read documentary collections across political boundaries, documentary cultures, and linguistic divides with a special focus on Ottoman and Safavid chanceries and how they interacted among themselves and/ or with the bureaucracies of the Republic of Venice, the Portuguese, and the Russian empires."[33]

As exciting as is the above description, and the opportunity it offers, for a medievalist who is also a globalist, engaged by comparative studies across barriers of time and space, it would be daunting to anyone not willing to do the language study, as also the mental gymnastics, required to understand, then benefit from the exacting protocols of this pedagogical initiative.

While one could argue that a program such as this will have a limited impact within a small scholarly subfield, it nonetheless augurs a double change toward the ICS. First, it asserts a Persianate accent throughout the Eurasian ecumene in the late middle early modern

period (15th–19th century), showing a network of connections linking chanceries thought to be solely European with those originating
from West Asia or the Middle East. Second, it uses the overall category of Balkans-to-Bengal, introduced by Shahab Ahmed in *What
Is Islam?* (2016),[34] to rethink the role of chanceries and bureaucracies
in a Persianate world that crosses imperial boundaries, as also cultural and linguistic divides. In effect, there is a priority to governance models rather than religious or academic orthodoxies, opening
the way for other fertile instances of in-between thinking or *barzakh* logic. While one awaits the early appearance of essays from this
2019 workshop on Persianate Eurasia, they will not likely be revised,
edited, and published before 2024.

Notes

1 I am indebted to Professor Carl W. Ernst for alerting me to this
   initiative in June 2020. Its larger elaboration can be found online
   at: https://medium.com/@openiti/openiti-aocp-9802865a6586
   (accessed November 10, 2020).
2 For several examples, see my 2015 public talk at the Franklin Institute
   of the Humanities, https://humanitiesfutures.org/papers/islamicate-
   cosmopolitan-past-without-future-future-still-unfolding. There is
   also much more to explore in the Mughal period, as announced in
   Valerie Gonzalez, *Aesthetic Hybridity in Mughal Painting, 1526–1658*
   (London: Routledge, 2016). Gonzalez' monograph was only brought
   to my attention in the final stages of my manifesto, through a reference in the recent, most accessible general introduction to Islamicate
   civilization across the Indian Ocean, Chiara Formichi, *Islam and Asia:
   A History* (Cambridge: Cambridge University Press, 2020): 63–65.
   Formichi underscores how Persian, Turkish, Arab, and Chinese
   styles "seeped through in modern Mughal-Persianate artistic styles,"
   reinforcing the eclectic, centripetal power of the ICS.
3 Gülru Necipoğlu, "The Concept of Islamic Art: Inherited Discourses and New Approaches," *Journal of Art Historiography* 6 (June,
   2016), 11.

4   Finbarr Barry Flood and Gülru Necipoğlu, eds., *A Companion to Islamic Art and Architecture* (Chichester, England: Wiley-Blackwell, 2017): 6. In the above citation from *A Companion to Islamic Art and Architecture*, vol. 1 (2017): 35, n. 10, the relevant author/title is listed as: Phillip B. Wagoner, "'Sultan among Hindu Kings': Dress, Titles, and the Islamicization of Hindu Culture at Vijayanagara," *Journal of Asian Studies* 554(4) (1996), 853–855. The actual pagination for the Wagoner article is: 851–880. It is a 29-page not a 3-page article, and more important than the length is its content. Wagoner paid close attention to Hodgson's argument for "Islamicate" as an alternative to "Islamic" on p. 851, and then elaborated that distinction in the rest of the article. Wagoner also introduces the distinction between "Islamicization" and "Islamization"; the former, unlike the latter, reflects cultural interactions and derivative usage not explicit embrace of Islam or allegiance to Muslim scriptural, liturgical, or juridical norms. Richard M. Eaton also affirms the Islamicate difference from its predecessors, "Muslim" and "Islamic." Eaton underscores what has been often said elsewhere: the term Islamicate was "intended to capture a broader, more flexible, and less communal notion of culture than is conveyed by the more narrowly defined religious terms 'Muslim' or 'Islamic.'" See Richard M. Eaton, ed., *India's Islamic Traditions, 711–1750* (New Delhi: Oxford University Press, 2003): 13.

5   The conference at which it was delivered was convened at Duke University in 1995, with John F. Richards and I the co-conveners. The essays from that lively gathering were subsequently published as *Beyond Turk and Hindu: Rethinking Religious Identities in Islamicate South Asia*, edited by David Gilmartin and Bruce B. Lawrence (Gainesville, FL: University Press of Florida, 2000). Wagoner's abbreviated essay, published as "Harihara, Bukka, and the Sultan: The Delhi Sultanate in the Political Imagination of Vijayanagara" (pp. 300–326), also stresses how Hindu kings in South India "vividly proclaimed their willingness to borrow the political discourse of Islamicate civilization" and at the same time "to borrow cultural forms and practices that have nothing to do with religion, but pertain to the sphere of secular courtly culture" (p. 316). It is important to stress that these norms were as much perceptual as visual, sensory rather than solely material. In reviewing the nature of the Vijayanagar buildings, Eaton

registers a surprising verdict: he claims them not to be Islamicate because they are "Islamic structures enclaved in an Indian world" but it is precisely the interchange of these diverse structural elements by Muslims and Hindus that qualifies their sensibility, or standards of taste, as "Islamicate," according to the definition of Islamicate Eaton himself provided (compare Richard M. Eaton, *India in the Persianate Age 1000–1075* (London: Penguin Books, 2019): 63–64 with Eaton (2003): 13).

6   Wagoner (2000): 855.

7   Wendy M.K. Shaw, *What is "Islamic" Art? Between Religion and Perception* (Cambridge: Cambridge University Press, 2019). I am indebted to Shaun Swanick for drawing my attention to this far-reaching and revisionist monograph.

8   Shaw (2019): 325.

9   Shaw (2019): 10.

10 Shaw (2019): x. See the Overview, pp. 6–9.

11 For a full statement of purpose, see the online declaration at https://brill.com/view/journals/ihiw/ihiw-overview.xml. There is a further book series, also published by Brill, with a similar title: *Islamicate Intellectual History: Studies and Texts in the Late Medieval and Early Modern periods*. It has published five monographs since 2015, and boasts a distinguished editorial board, including Judith Pfeiffer, Shahzad Bashir, and Heidrun Eichner.

12 Salvatore (2018): 22–23, here excerpted and modified to fit the overview of this chapter. It is important to stress that this is a radically revisionist view of the ebb and flow, the centering and marginalizing, of Islamicate elements in world history. It sets the stage for a fresh rethinking of hemispheric history, privileging but also expanding Hodgsonian initiatives. One of the co-editors of *The Wiley-Blackwell History of Islam* is Babak Rahimi, and Rahimi has also co-edited a special issue on "Early Modern Islamic Cities" in the *Journal for Early Modern Cultural Studies* 18(3) (Summer, 2018), with several contributions that offer multiple insights into the ICS. Yet the South Asian segment is repeatedly described as Southeast Asian, again reflecting the lack of engagement with the Indian Ocean as a major theater for Islamicate networks, influences, and trajectories. See https://muse.jhu.edu/article/732786 (accessed November 8, 2020)

As with many other late additions elsewhere in my text and foot-notes, I am indebted to an avid outside reader for this reference that would otherwise have escaped me.

13   A.C.S. Peacock and D.G. Tor, eds., *Medieval Central Asia and the Per-sianate World: Iranian Tradition and Islamic Civilization* (London: IB Tauris, 2015): 24–25.

14   Michael Feener review of A.C.S. Peacock, ed., *Islamisation: Compara-tive Perspectives from History* (Edinburgh: Edinburgh University Press, 2017) in *Journal of Islamic Studies* 30(1) (January, 2019), 108–111.

15   In his seminal article Wagoner also introduces the distinction bet-ween "Islamicization" and "Islamization" in order to stress that the former, unlike the latter, reflects cultural interactions and derivative usage not explicit embrace of Islam or allegiance to Muslim scrip-tural, liturgical, or juridical norms. He expresses regret that the two terms sound too much alike to be readily distinguishable for the casual reader (Wagoner (2000): 855).

16   All scholars who have worked with Hodgson, or based their schol-arship on his, have noted—what one calls—"his quest to purify scholarly terminology." See Douglas E. Streusand, *The Formation of the Mughal Empire* (Bombay, India: Oxford University Press, 1989): 21. Hodgson never viewed his neologisms as definitive choices, but rather as heuristic devices, prompting Streusand, with other Indolo-gists, including Eaton, to think of "the Mughals" not as latter day Mongols, which "Mughals" connotes, but rather as descendants of Timur, hence, Timurids or Indo-Timurids (Marshall Hodgson, *The Venture of Islam* (Chicago, IL: University of Chicago Press, 1974): 3, n. 62).

17   Abbas Amanat and Assef Ashraf, eds., *The Persianate World: Rethinking a Shared Sphere* (Leiden/Boston, MA: Brill, 2019).

18   Assef Ashraf in the introduction to Amanat and Ashraf (2019): 8–9.

19   "There was no recognition of a geopolitical construct called the Middle East in any Persian, Arabic, or Turkish geographical or his-torical texts, or in any informed European Orientalist sources before World War II" (Amanat, "Remembering the Persianate" in Amanat and Ashraf (2019): 61).

20   Brian Spooner, "Epilogue: the Persianate Millennium" in Nile Green, ed., *The Persianate World: The Frontiers of a Eurasian Lingua Franca*

(Oakland: University of California Press, 2019): 314–315. Spooner's assessment, here summarized, rings the death knell on Persianate futures, yet Spooner, together with William Hanaway, has contributed one of the major volumes on the literary legacy of the Persianate world. See Brian Spooner and William L. Hanaway, eds., *Literacy in the Persianate World: Writing and the Social Order* (Philadelphia, PA: University of Pennsylvania Press, 2012). It is the outcome of his argument not the documentary benefit of his research that I am concerned to highlight.

21   This process of narrowing rather than expanding the vision of citizens in the modern nation-state of Iran has been charted in Amanat (2019): 58–59. While the analysis is accurate, the optimism is less convincing, owing to the dire downward trend in humanistic studies generally but also the literary range of area studies, even in Western Europe much less "remote" regions of the ecumene. Also notable, and regrettable, is the loss of Persianate influence even among South Asian Muslim elites in the late 20th/early 21st century. That decline is epitomized by Green at the end of his long, informed introduction to *The Persianate World*: "it is worth taking stock of the scale of Persianate literary eclipse by way of a bibliographical statistic from the library of a twentieth-century South Asian Muslim. Among the several thousand books collected by Jamal al-Din 'Abd al-Wahhab (1919–2012), 55% were in Urdu, 30% in Arabic, 10% in English, and a mere 5% in Persian. Even for this religious scholar, educated in the great Farangi Mahal madrasa founded under Mughal patronage, Persian had been sidelined by other, national, religious, and imperial languages" (p. 55).

22   Attention to trade, economics, and politics was cited by Ashraf as a need for all studies of the late middle Islamicate empires (Ashraf (2019): 10), yet as Kinra counterargues, the weight of cultural history, at the heart of Persianate studies, remains an even more essential priority.

23   Rajeev Kinra, *Writing Self, Writing Empire: Chandar Bhan Brahman and the Cultural World of the Indo-Persian State Secretary* (Oakland, CA: University of California Press, 2015): 12–13.

24   Kinra (2015): 206.

25   Green (2019): xiv.

26 Green (2019): 2.

27 Green (2019): 4.

28 Another recent monograph that underscores the limits of nationalist history and the benefits of *adab* as a transnational, multicultural ethos is Mana Kia, *Persianate Selves: Memories of Place and Origin Before Nationalism* (Stanford, CA: Stanford University Press, 2020). The book appeared too late to be woven into my own narrative about Persianate longing, but this passage captures the tone of my argument: "Before nationalism, Persianate selves could hail from many places, and their origins comprised a variety of lineages. The interrelations among these lineages render coherent their multiple modes of imagination, practice, and experience," and the linchpin of this multiplicity, harking back to the poet Hafiz, was *adab*, "the proper form of things, as the means and manifestation of the most harmonious, beautiful, and virtuous substance, most perfect and closest to the Truth." In short, *adab* evoked and embodied both Persianate as well as Islamicate vistas of the transcendent (pp. 70–71).

29 Green (2019): 17. There follows in the full introduction to Green's edited volume a synopsis of each of the chapters as well as their collective value in both instantiating and expanding Hodgson's vision of a Persianate zone/world. What is provided here are just some of the highlights relevant to evaluating Persianate studies.

30 Green (2019): 21. The importance of chanceries continues to be stressed in scholarship on the arc of Persianate influence throughout the Afro-Asian ecumene. See Kinra (2015) for one of the major case studies in late Mughal, early modern South Asia.

31 See Ronit Ricci, *Islam Translated: Literature, Conversion, and the Arabic Cosmopolis of South and Southeast Asia* (Chicago, CA: University of Chicago Press, 2011). In chapter 9, "the Arabic Cosmopolis of South and Southeast Asia," she writes about "shifting cosmopolitanisms" since the Arabic cosmopolis of South and Southeast Asia "was never a singular entity in the region: overlapping, waxing and waning cosmopolitan worlds existed and were not mutually exclusive" (p. 267). It would resonate as well as contrast with the Arabicate Zone of Africa etched by Green in his essay "*From 'Persianate Zone' to 'Persianate World': Thinking with Hodgson Fifty Years On*" for the Yale Law School 2018 Conference.

32 See n. 27.

33 The description here abbreviated can be found in its original form at H-Net, itself an international interdisciplinary organization of scholars and teachers, founded in 1994 and dedicated to developing the educational potential of the Internet and the World Wide Web. See: https://networks.h-net.org/node/73374/announcements/3531264/call-applications-summer-school-cultures-documentation.

34 Shahab Ahmed, *What Is Islam?: The Importance of Being Islamic* (Princeton, NJ: Princeton University Press, 2016).

Conclusion

In the final analysis, academic labor remains the major window for the restive, resilient eruption of Islamicate Cosmopolitan Spirit (ICS). Institutional options limit the horizon of possibility: since there is not, nor will there soon be, a Persianate studies initiative, similar to Middle East and Central, South, and Southeast Asian studies, as also Islamic and Jewish studies, Islamicate endeavors will be suspended between different units, disciplines, and research agendas. In terms of academic orphanage, Eastern Christianity might be the closest parallel, though in its scope and scale the arc of a Persianate cosmopolis, at the heart of the ICS, is broader, more varied, and more productive than its Eastern Christian counterpart.

While the future influence of an ICS may not be clear yet, for either academics or the public at large, it does have more opportunity now than at any point in the late 20th or early 21st century. Especially due to the recent turn toward reconsidering the literary production of the high cultural past of Islamicate civilization, it seems possible to assert that building blocks for an ICS are not only in place but also expanding. Here are its foundational brick and mortar parts. They are twofold: terminological and constructive.

Islamicate Cosmopolitan Spirit, First Edition. Bruce B. Lawrence.
© 2021 Bruce B. Lawrence. Published 2021 by John Wiley & Sons, Ltd.

The first requirement is revisionism. Revisionism in basic terminology is at once necessary and ongoing: what Hodgson began did not, and should not, end with him, but it also cannot ignore his seminal insights. Islamicate is crucial because it is neither secular nor creedal; it is instead a spiritual elan filtered through cultural practices and artifacts; the transcendent, far from being absent, is defined as a multilingual, transnational resource. Allied with Islamicate is cosmopolitan, also redefined and broadly applied. Cosmopolitan is not limited to one area, one time, or one social unit. The polis or Greek city gave it its second syllable, but it is the first syllable, cosmos, that confirms how the vertical not only meshes with the horizontal but also redefines it. Cosmopolitan is always an aspiration, as much longing for the just and beautiful (*ihsan*) through vigilant deportment (*adab*), as it is belonging—whether to a region, a town, or city, an empire or nation.[1] But also critical is Spirit. Spirit is the motivating impetus for all that is, and all who are, Islamicate cosmopolitan. Spirit is at once restless and boundless. It resists stasis and reification but also opposes violence, either physical or systemic. It is more evident in contexts that are fluid, at once multilingual and multiethnic, rather than those that are monolingual and ethnically divided.

And so, the second requirement is historical retelling of the past but also engaging the present and imaging anew the future. History revisited and revised will reveal the ICS pervasive during the premodern period, especially in the Eastern hemisphere of Afro-Eurasia, from the Balkans to Bengal to Mindanao, across the Indian Ocean and into the Pacific. The forces of change that prioritized a Western ascent—including Russia and Japan, along with Europe and America as major players—have now made the ICS less evident, its contour and impact more difficult to trace. Although digital technology may help reduce the gap of understanding, it is the contours of Islamicate civilization that need to be rethought using fuzzy or *barzakh* logic. Let our vision of the planet expand and deepen. Recognize the connectedness of what Hodgson called the Afro-Eurasian ecumene. It allows us to appreciate a multiplicity of fluctuating patterns, in-betweens, middle processes that make history far more gray than black or white, as has been the case with too many scholarly works on Islam. Especially important is the performance of ethical practices (*adab*), at once invisible and invincible, that pervade the ICS.[2] They reveal the agility of language and the mobility of texts across the multiple zones of Islamicate civilization. Boundaries as performances are porous, and so are the people who traverse them in the search of possible worlds. *Adab* needs to be coupled with *taskhir*. Together they mark the ICS as both embodied praxis and episteme for actions, troubling the notion that there is a single or singular Islamic perspective, tradition or life world. And it is the living practices of Islam that remain crucial to understanding how the ICS works. Above all, it foregrounds networks of artists, historians, scholars, and poets to patch together a large quilt of interwoven small histories, providing a new planetary vision that simultaneously deemphasizes regional or linguistic essentialism and stresses instead a fuzzy, *barzakh* logic conjoining religion and culture.

One can be confident that ICS will remain at the intersection of multiple audiences, both friendly and hostile. Never destined to be a core focus of the academy or a priority for the general public, ICS will nonetheless persist, accenting the fungible nature of *barzakh* logic. Neither East or West, premodern or modern, encompassing all opposites while yielding to none, it illumines an interstitial domain, open to the curious and the intrepid alike. It beckons us to a future still unfolding.

Notes

1 In addition to the edited volumes on Southeast Asia earlier cited, also noteworthy is Robert Rozehnal, ed., *Piety, Politics, and Everyday Ethics in Southeast Asian Islam: Beautiful Behavior* (London and New York, NY: Bloomsbury, 2019). "Beautiful behavior" in the subtitle is an English rendition for *adab*, and in this elegant volume it is demonstrated how musical performance, like environmental ethics, crisscrosses ethnic, racial, and linguistic boundaries in the quest for what

is right and good and beautiful, the epitome of Islamicate norms and values.

2 Among several instances of *adab* as performance in the Persianate realm not already discussed are those chronicled and examined in Lloyd Ridgeon, ed., *Javanmardi: The Ethics and Practice of Persianate Perfection* (London: Gingko Library, 2018), with case studies from Anatolia, Armenia, and Central Asia as well as modern-day Iran and Turkey. Again, I am grateful to an outside reviewer for bringing this edited volume to my attention; the scope of *adab*, like the ICS, exceeds the grasp of a single monograph, even the most ambitious manifesto.

Bibliography

I Cosmopolitanism—Theory

Ackerman, B. 1994 "Rooted Cosmopolitanism," *Ethics* 104(3): 516–535.

Appiah, Kwame Anthony 2006 *Cosmopolitanism: Ethics in a World of Strangers*. New York, NY: W.W. Norton & Company.

Appiah, Kwame Anthony 2005 *The Ethics of Identity*. Princeton, NJ: Princeton University Press.

Archibugi, Daniele 2003 "A Critical Analysis of the Self-Determination of Peoples: A Cosmopolitan Perspective," *Constellations* 10(4): 488–505.

Badiou, Alain 2001 *Ethics: An Essay on the Understanding of Evil* (tr., P. Hallward). London and New York, NY: Verso.

Badiou, Alain 2005 *Metapolitics* (tr., R. Brassier). London and New York, NY: Verso.

Bailliet, Cecilia and Katja Franko Aas, eds. 2011 *Cosmopolitan Justice and Its Discontents*. Abingdon, England: Routledge.

Bauman, Zygmund 1998 "On Glocalization: Or Globalization for Some, Localization for Some Others," *Thesis Eleven* 54: 37–50.

Bauman, Zygmund 2002 "The Fate of Humanity in the Posy-Trinitarian World," *Journal of Human Rights* 1(3): 283–303.

Beck, Ulrich 2002 "The Cosmopolitan Perspective: Sociology in the Second Age of Modernity" in Steven Vertovec and Robin Cohen,

Islamicate Cosmopolitan Spirit, First Edition. Bruce B. Lawrence.

eds. *Conceiving Cosmopolitanism: Theory, Context, and Practice*. Oxford: Oxford University Press, 61–85.

Beck, Ulrich 2004 "Cosmopolitan Realism: On the Distinction Between Cosmopolitanism in Philosophy and the Social Sciences," *Global Networks* 4(2): 131–156.

Beck, Ulrich and Edgar Grande 2010 "Varieties of Second Modernity: The Cosmopolitan Turn in Social and Political Theory and Research," *British Journal of Sociology* 61(3): 409–443.

Benhabib, Seyla 2002 *The Claims of Culture: Equality and Diversity in the Global Era*. Princeton, NJ: Princeton University Press.

Benhabib, Seyla 2004 *The Rights of Others: Aliens, Residents and Citizens*. Cambridge: Cambridge University Press.

Benhabib, Seyla 2006 *Another Cosmopolitanism*. Oxford: Oxford University Press.

Bhabha, Homi 1996 "Unsatisfied: Notes on Vernacular Cosmopolitanism" in Laura Garcia-Moreno and Peter C. Pfeiffer, eds. *Text and Nation: Cross-Disciplinary Essays on Cultural and National Identities*. Columbia, SC: Camden House, 191–207.

Bhabha, Homi 2000 "The Vernacular Cosmopolitan" in Ferdinand Dennis and Naseem Khan, eds. *Voices of the Crossing: The Impact of Britain on Writers from Asia, the Caribbean, and Africa*. London: Serpent's Tail, 133–142.

Bose, Sugata and Kris Manjapra 2010 *Cosmopolitan Thought Zones: South Asia and the Global Circulation of Ideas*. Basingstoke and New York, NY: Palgrave Macmillan.

Brennan, Tim 1989 "Cosmopolitans and Celebrities," *Race and Class* 31(1): 1–19.

Brennan, Tim 1997 *At Home in the World: Cosmopolitanism Now*. Cambridge, MA: Harvard University Press.

Brennan, Tim 2001 "Cosmopolitanism and Internationalism," *New Left Review* 7(Jan–Feb): 75–85.

Brown, Garrett Wallace and David Held 2010 *The Cosmopolitanism Reader*. Cambridge: Polity.

Calhoun, Craig 2002 "The Class Consciousness of Frequent Travellers: Towards a Critique of Actually Existing Cosmopolitanism" in Steven Vertovec and Robin Cohen, eds. *Conceiving Cosmopolitanism: Theory, Context, and Practice*. New York, NY: Oxford University Press, 86–109.

Calhoun, Craig 2008 "Cosmopolitanism and Nationalism," *Nations and Nationalism* 14(3): 427–448.

Cerwonka, Allaine and Llisa H. Malki 2007 *Improvising Theory: Process and Temporality in Ethnographic Fieldwork*. Chicago, IL: University of Chicago Press.

Chakrabarty, Dipesh 2000 "Universalism and Belonging in the Logic of Capital," *Public Culture* 12(3): 653–678.

Davis, Diane E. and Nora Libertun de Duren, eds. 2011 *Cities and Sovereignty: Identity Politics in Urban Spaces*. Bloomington, IN: Indiana University Press.

Dawson, Andrew 2006 "The Cosmopolitan Imagination: Critical Cosmopolitanism and Social Theory," *British Journal of Sociology* 57(1): 25–47.

Delanty, Gerard, ed. 2012 *Routledge Handbook of Cosmopolitan Studies*. London and New York, NY: Routledge.

Demerdash, Nancy 2012 "Consuming Revolution: Ethics, Art and Ambivalence in the Arab Spring," *New Middle Eastern Studies* 2: 1–18.

Derrida, Jacques 2001 *On Cosmopolitanism and Forgiveness*. London and New York, NY: Routledge.

Dobson, Andrew 2006 "Thick Cosmopolitanism," *Political Studies* 54: 165–184.

Dussel, Enrique 1993 "Eurocentrism and Modernity," *Boundary 2* 20(3): 65–76.

Dussel, Enrique 2001 "The Sociohistorical Meaning of Liberation Theology (Reflections about Its Origin and World Context)" in David N. Hopkins et al., eds. *Religions/Globalizations: Theories and Cases*. Durham, NC: Duke University, 34–35.

Giri, A.K. 2006 "Cosmopolitanism and Beyond: Towards a Multiverse of Transformations," *Development and Change* 37(6): 1277–1292.

Godrej, Farah 2011 *Cosmopolitan Political Thought: Method, Practice, Discipline*. New York, NY: Oxford University Press.

González-Ruibal, Alfredo 2009 "Vernacular Cosmopolitanism: An Archeological Critique of Universalistic Reason" in Lynn Meskell, ed. *Cosmopolitan Archaeologies*. Durham, NC: Duke University Press, 113–139.

Graebner, David 2002 "Names beyond Nations: The Making of Local Cosmopolitans," *Etudes Rurales* 163(164): 215–232.

Graebner, David 2008 "On Cosmopolitanism and (Vernacular) Democratic Creativity: Or, There Never Was a West" in Pnina

Werbner, ed. *Anthropology and the New Cosmopolitanism: Rooted, Feminist and Vernacular Perspectives.* Oxford: Berg, 281–305.

Habermas, Jurgen 1998 "Learning by Disaster? A Diagnostic Look Back on the Short 20th Century," *Constellations* 5(3): 307–320.

Hansen, David T. 2008a "Curriculum and the Idea of a Cosmopolitan Inheritance," *Journal of Curriculum Studies* 40(3): 289–312.

Hansen, David T. 2008b "Education Viewed Through a Cosmopolitan Prism," *Philosophy of Education Yearbook*: 206–214.

Hansen, David T. 2010 "Chasing Butterflies Without a Net: Interpreting Cosmopolitanism," *Studies in Philosophy and Education* 29: 151–166.

Hansen, David T. 2011 *The Teacher and the World: A Study of Cosmopolitanism as Education.* New York, NY: Routledge.

Harvey, David 2001 "Cosmopolitanism and the Banality of Geographical Evils," *Public Culture* 12(2): 529–564.

Held, David 1995a *Democracy and the Global Order: From the Modern State to Cosmopolitan Governance.* Cambridge: Polity.

Held, David 1995b "Democracy and the International Order" in Daniele Archibugi and David Held, eds. *Cosmopolitan Democracy: An Agenda for a New World Order.* Cambridge: Polity, 96–120.

Held, David 2003 "Cosmopolitanism: Globalisation Tamed?," *Review of International Studies* 29: 465–480.

Hollinger, David A. 1995 *Postethnic America: Beyond Multiculturalism.* New York, NY: Basic Books.

Hollinger, David A. 2006 *Cosmopolitanism and Solidarity: Studies in Ethnoracial, Religious, and Professional Affiliation in the United States.* Madison, WI: University of Wisconsin Press.

Johnson, Mark and Mattia Eumanti 2012 *Vernacular Cosmopolitans in an Age of Anxiety.* Conference at Nanterre University, France July 10,2012.

Kaldor, Mary 2002 "Cosmopolitanism and Organized Violence" in Steven Vertovec and Robin Cohen, eds. *Conceiving Cosmopolitanism: Theory, Context, Practice.* New York: NY: Oxford University Press, 268–278.

Kendell, Gavin, Ian Woodward, and Zlato Skrbis 2009 *The Sociology of Cosmopolitanism: Globalization, Identity, Culture and Government.* New York, NY: Palgrave Macmillan.

Kosko, Bart and Michael Toms 1993 *Fuzzy Thinking: The New Science of Fuzzy Logic.* Westport, CT: Hyperion.

Bibliography

Majid, Anouar 2000 *Unveiling Traditions: Postcolonial Islam in a Polycentric World*. Durham, NC: Duke University Press.

Meskell, Lynn, ed. 2009 *Cosmopolitan Archaeologies*. Durham, NC: Duke University Press.

Mignolo, Walter 2000 "The Many Faces of Cosmo-polis: Border Thinking and Critical Cosmopolitanism," *Public Culture* 12(3): 721–748.

Mignolo, Walter 2008 "Who Speaks for the 'Human' in Human Rights?" in Taieb Belghazi et al. *Who Can Act for the Human?* Rabat: Mohammed V University Colloque set Seminars no. 151.: 227–248.

Mignolo, Walter 2011 "Cosmopolitan Localisms: Overcoming Colonial and Imperial Differences" in *The Darker Side of Western Modernity: Global Futures, Decolonial Options*. Durham, NC: Duke University Press, 252–294.

Nussbaum, Martha C. 1994 "Patriotism and Cosmopolitanism," Boston Review.http://bostonreview.net/martha-nussbaum-patriotism-and-cosmopolitanism

Nussbaum, Martha C. 2019 *The Cosmopolitan Tradition: A Noble but Flawed Ideal*. Cambridge, MA: Harvard University Press.

Papastephanou, Marianna 2012 *Thinking Differently about Cosmopolitanism: Theory, Eccentricity, and the Globalized World*. Boulder and London: Paradigm Publishers.

Picard, David and Sonja Buchberger 2014 *Couchsurfing Cosmopolitanisms: Can Tourism Make a Better World?* Bielefeld, Germany:Transcript-Verlag.

Pollock, Sheldon, Homi K. Bhabha, Carol A. Breckenridge, and Dipesh Chakrabarty 2002 "Cosmopolitanisms" in Carol A. Breckensridge et al., eds. *Cosmopolitanism*. Durham, NC: Duke University Press, 1–14.

Pleyers, Geoffrey 2011 *Alter-Globalization: Becoming Actors in a Global Age*. Cambridge: Polity.

Rapport, Nigel 2007 "An Outline for Cosmopolitan Study," *Current Anthropology* 48(2): 257–283.

Salto, N. and P. Standish 2008 "Transcending Borders from Within: Stanley Cavell and the Politics of Interpretation." Paper presented at the International Conference on Cosmopolitanism, Stockholm, Sweden.

Sennett, Richard 2002 "Cosmopolitanism and the Social Experience of the City" in Steven Vertovec and Robin Cohen, eds. *Conceiving Cosmopolitanism: Theory, Context, and Practice*. New York, NY: Oxford University Press, 42–47.

Bibliography

Shail, Mayaram, ed. 2008 *The Other Global City: Living Together in Asia.* London and New York, NY: Routledge.

Tlostanova, Madina V. and Walter D. Mignolo 2012 *Learning to Unlearn: Decolonial Reflections from Eurasia and the Americas.* Columbus, OH: Ohio State University Press.

Trouillot, Michel-Rolph 2002 *Critically Modern: Alternatives, Alterities, Anthropologies.* Bloomington, IN: Indiana University Press.

Vertovec, Steven 2010 "Cosmopolitanism" in Kim Knott and Sean McLoughlin, eds. *Diasporas: Concepts, Intersections, Identities.* London: Zed, 63–68

Vertovec, Steven and Robin Cohen 2002 "Introduction: Conceiving Cosmopolitanism" in *Conceiving Cosmopolitansim: Theory, Context and Practice.* New York and London: Oxford University Press, 1–24.

Werbner, Pnina, ed. 2008 *Anthropology and the New Cosmopolitanism: Rooted, Feminist and Vernacular Perspectives.* Oxford: Berg.

II Islamicate Cosmopolitan

Alatas, Syed Farid and Abdolreza Alami, eds. 2018 *The Civilisational and Cultural Heritage of Iran and the Malay World: A Cultural Discourse.* Kuala Lumpur: Gerakbudaya Enterprise, Selangor, Malaysia and Cultural Centre, Embassy of the Islamic Republic of Iran.

Alavi, Seema 2011 "Siddiq Hasan Khan (1832–90) and the Creation of a Muslim Cosmopolitanism in the 19th Century," *Journal of the Economic and Social History of the Orient* 54(1): 1–38.

Alavi, Seema 2015 *Muslim Cosmopolitanism in the Age of Empire.* Cambridge, MA: Harvard University Press.

Aljunied, Khairudin 2017 *Muslim Cosmopolitanism: Southeast Asian Islam in Comparative Perspective.* Edinburgh: Edinburgh University Press.

Alkhateeb, Firas 2014 *Lost Islamic History: Reclaiming Muslim Civilization from the Past.* London: Hurst & Company.

Allawi, Ali A. 2010 *The Crisis of Islamic Civilization.* New Haven, CT: Yale University Press.

Amanat, Abbas and Assef Ashraf, eds. 2019 *The Persianate World: Rethinking a Shared Sphere.* Leiden and Boston, MA: Brill.

Baer, Marc 2007 "Globalization, Cosmopolitanism, and the Donme in Ottoman Salonica and Turkish Istanbul," *Journal of World History* 18(2): 141–170.

Baker, Felicitas 2008 "Cosmopolitanism beyond the Towns: Rural-Urban Relations on the Southern Swahili Coast in the Twentieth Century" in Edward Simpson and Kai Kreese, eds. *Struggling with History: Islam and Cosmopolitanism in the Western Indian Ocean.* New York, NY: Columbia Press, 261–290.

Balabanlilar, Lisa 2012 *Imperial Identity in the Mughal Empire: Memory and Dynastic Politics in Early Modern South and Central Asia.* London and New York, NY: I.B. Tauris.

Bang, Anne K. 2008 "Cosmopolitanism Colonised? Three Cases from Zanzibar 1890-1920" in Edward Simpson and Kai Kreese, eds. *Struggling with History: Islam and Cosmopolitanism in the Western Indian Ocean.* New York, NY: Columbia Press, 167–188.

Barletta, Vincent 2005 *Covert Gestures: Crypto-Islamic Literature as Cultural Practice in Early Modern Spain.* Minneapolis, MN: University of Minnesota Press.

Bayat, Asef, 2010 "Everyday Cosmopolitanism" in Asef Bayat, ed. *Life as Politics: How Ordinary People Change the Middle East.* Stanford, CA: Stanford University Press,185–208.

Becker, Felicitas 2012 "Freeborn Villagers: Islam and the Local Uses of Cosmopolitan Connections in the Tanzanian Countryside" in Derryl N. MacLean and Sikeena Karmali Ahmed, eds. *Cosmopolitanisms in Muslim Contexts: Perspectives from the Past.* Edinburgh: Edinburgh University Press, 10–30.

Becker, Felicitas 2008 "Cosmopolitanism beyond the Towns: Rural-Urban Relations on the Southern Swahili Coast in the Twentieth Century" in Edward Simpson and Kai Kreese, eds. *Struggling with History: Islam and Cosmopolitanism in the Western Indian Ocean.* New York, NY: Columbia Press, 261–290.

Belghazi, Taieb 2001 "The Mediterranean(s), *Barzakh,* Event" in T. Belghazi and L. Haddad, eds. *Global/Local Cultures and Sustainable Development.* Rabat: Faculty of Letters and Human Sciences, Mohammed V University; 217–223.

Belghazi, Taieb, et al. 2008 *Who Can Act for the Human?* Rabat: Mohammed V University et colloques Seminars no 151.

Belghazi, Taiebwith Mohamed Ezroura 2008 "Shifting Topographies for the Human" in *Who Can Act for the Human?* Rabat: Mohammed V University et colloques Seminars no 151: 17–29.

131

Campbell, Gwyn, 2008 "Islam in Indian Ocean Africa Prior to the Scramble" in Edward Simpson and Kai Kreese, eds. *Struggling with History: Islam and Cosmopolitanism in the Western Indian Ocean*. New York, NY: Columbia Press, 43–92.

Canuday, (Jose) Jowel 2012 "Embodying Cosmopolitanism: Dance Heritage, Music Videos, and the Embrace of Global Imaginaries in Sulu and Zamboanga (Mindanao, the Southern Philippines)" paper presented at conference at Nanterre on "Vernacular Cosmopolitanisms in an Age of Anxiety," July, organizers, Mark Johnson and Mattia Fumanti.

Canuday, (Jose) Jowel 2013 "Music, Dances, and Videos: Identity Making and the Cosmopolitan Imagination in the Southern Philippines," DPhil Dissertation, Oxford University.

Canuday, (Jose) Jowel 2018 "Re-visioning Obscure Spaces: Enduring Cosmopolitanism in the Sulu Archipelago and Zamboanga Peninsula" *Thesis Eleven* 145(1): 77–98.

cooke, miriam 1984 "Ibn Khaldun and Language: From Linguistic Habit to Philological Craft" in Bruce B. Lawrence, ed. *Ibn Khaldun and Islamic Ideology*. Leiden, the Netherlands: Brill, 27–36.

cooke, miriam 2007 "Muslimwoman Cosmopolitanism," the second keynote address at The Association of Muslim Social Scientists (AMSS), Third Annual Canadian Regional Conference on "Cosmopolitan Islamic Identity and Thought" at Wilfrid Laurier University,Waterloo, Ontario.

cooke, miriam 2014 *Tribal Modern: Branding New Nations in the Arab Gulf*. Berkeley, CA: University of California Press.

cooke, miriam and Bruce B. Lawrence, eds. 2005 *Muslim Networks from Hajj to Hip-Hop*. Chapel Hill, NC: University of North Carolina Press.

cooke, miriam, Erdag Göknar, and Grant Parker, eds. 2008 *Mediterranean Passages: Readings from Dido to Derrida*. Chapel Hill, NC: University of North Carolina.

Cornell, Vincent J. 2005 "Ibn Battuta's Opportunism: The Networks and Loyalties of a Medieval Muslim Scholar" in miriam cooke and Bruce B. Lawrence, eds. *Muslim Networks from Hajj to Hip-Hop*. Chapel Hill, NC: University of North Carolina Press, 31–50.

Dadi, Iftikhar 2012 "Abdur Rahman Chughtai: Cosmopolitan Mughal Aesthetic in the Age of Print" in Derryl N. MacLean and Sikeena Karmali Ahmed, eds. *Cosmopolitanisms in Muslim Contexts: Perspectives from the Past*. Edinburgh: Edinburgh University Press, 127–155.

Diouf, Mamadou 2000 "The Senagalese Murid Trade Diaspora and the Making of a Vernacular Cosmopolitanism," Translated by Steven Randall *Public Culture* 12(3): 679–702.

Driezen, Henk 2005 "Mediterranean Port Cities: Cosmopolitanism Reconsidered," *History and Anthropology* 16(1): 129–141.

Eaton, Richard M., ed. 2003 *India's Islamic Traditions, 711–1750*. New Delhi: Oxford University Press.

Eaton, Richard M. 2014 "Revisiting the Persian Cosmopolis," Asia Times July 19.

Eaton, Richard M. 2019a *India in the Persianate Age 1000–1075*. London: Penguin & Oakland, CA: University of California Press.

Eaton, Richard M. 2019b "The Persian Cosmopolis (900–1900) and the Sanskrit Cosmopolis (400–1400)" in Abbas Amanat and Assef Ashraf, eds. *The Persianate World: Rethinking a Shared Sphere*. Leiden, the Netherlands: Brill, 63–83.

Euben, Roxanne L. 2006 *Journeys to the Other Shore: Muslim and Western Travelers in Search of Knowledge*. Princeton, NJ: Princeton University Press.

Fathy, Hassan 1973/2004 *Architecture for the Poor*. Cairo: AUC Press.

Feyissa, Dereje and Bruce B. Lawrence 2014 "Muslims Renegotiating Marginality in Contemporary Ethiopia," *The Muslim World* 105(July): 281–305.

Flood, Finbarr Barry and Gülru Necipoğlu, eds. 2017 *A Companion to Islamic Art and Architecture*. Chichester, England: Wiley-Blackwell.

Formichi, Chiara 2020 *Islam and Asia: A History*. Cambridge: Cambridge University Press.

Frost, Mark Ravinder 2010 "In Search of Cosmopolitan Discourse: A Historical Journey across the Indian Ocean from Singapore to South Africa, 1870–1920" in Pamila Gupta, Isabel Hofmeyr, and M.N. Pearson, eds. *Eyes across the Water: Navigating the Indian Ocean*. Pretoria: Unisa Press.

Gedacht, Joshua and R. Michael Feener, eds. 2018 *Challenging Cosmopolitanism: Coercion, Mobility and Displacement in Islamic Asia*. Edinburgh: Edinburgh University Press.

George, Kenneth M. 2007 "Art and Identity Politics: Nation, Religion, Ethnicity, Elsewhere" in Kathryn Robinson, ed. *Asian and Pacific Cosmopolitans*. New York, NY: Palgrave, 37–59.

George, Kenneth M. 2009 "Ethics, Iconoclasm, and Qur'anic Art in Indonesia," *Cultural Anthropology* 24(4): 589–621.

George, Kenneth M. 2010 *Picturing Islam: Art and Ethics in a Muslim Lifeworld*. Chichester, England: Wiley-Blackwell.

Gilmartin, David and Bruce B. Lawrence, eds. 2000 *Beyond Turk and Hindu: Rethinking Religious Identities in Islamicate South Asia*. Gainesville, FL: University Press of Florida.

Gonzalez, Victoria 2016 *Aesthetic Hybridity in Mughal Painting*. London: Routledge.

Graiouid, Said 2011 *Communication and Everyday Performance: Public Space and the Public Sphere in Morocco*. Rabat: Faculty of Letters and Human Sciences, University Mohammed V. Series: Essays & Studies No 46.

Green, Nile 2012 "Kebabs and Port Wine: The Culinary Cosmopolitanism of Anglo-Persian Dining, 1800–1835" in Derryl N. MacLean and Sikeena Karmali Ahmed, eds. *Cosmopolitanisms in Muslim Contexts: Perspectives from the Past*. Edinburgh: Edinburgh University Press, 105–126.

Green, Nile 2018 *"From 'Persianate Zone' to 'Persianate World': Thinking with Hodgson Fifty Years On*. Conference paper, Yale Law School.

Green, Nile, ed. 2019a *The Persianate World: The Frontiers of a Eurasian Lingua Franca*. Oakland, CA: University of California Press.

Green, Nile 2019b "The Antipodes of 'Progress': A Journey to the End of Indo-Persian" in Abbas Amanat and Assef Ashraf, eds. *The Persianate World: Rethinking a Shared Sphere*. Leiden and Boston, MA: Brill.

Hanley, William 2012 "Cosmopolitan Cursing in Late Nineteenth Century Alexandria" in Derryl N. MacLean and Sikeena Karmali Ahmed, eds. *Cosmopolitanisms in Muslim Contexts: Perspectives from the Past*. Edinburgh: Edinburgh University Press, 92–104.

Hanley, William 2008 "Grieving Cosmopolitanism in Middle East Studies," *History Compass* 6(5) (2008): 1346–1367.

Hilarian, Larry Francis 2018 "The Persian and Arabian Musical and Cultural Impact on the Early Global Trade-Routes to *Lautan Melayu* (The Malay Sea)" in Syed Farid Alatas and Abdolreza Alami, eds. *The Civilisational and Cultural Heritage of Iran and the Malay World: A Cultural Discourse*, jointly published by Gerakbudaya Enterprise, Selangor, Malaysia and Cultural Centre, Embassy of the Islamic Republic of Iran, Kuala Lumpur, 15–38.

Ho, Engseng. 2006 *The Graves of Tarim: Genealogy and Mobility across the Indian Ocean*. Berkeley, CA: University of California Press.

Bibliography

Hoesterey, James B. April 2012 "Prophetic Cosmopolitanism" in Mara A. Leichtman and Dorothea Schulz, eds. *"Muslim Cosmopolitanism: Movement, Identity and Contemporary Reconfiguration"* Special issue of *City & Society* 24: 38–61.

Humphrey, Caroline, Magnus Marsden, and Vera Skirvskaja, 2008 "Cosmopolitanism and the City: Interaction and Co-existence in Bukhara" in Maryam Shail, ed. *The Other Global City: Living Together in Asia.* London: Routledge, 202–232).

Iqtidar, Humeira 2012 "Cosmopolitanism, Religion and Inter-civilizational Dialogue" in Delanty, et al. *Routledge Handbook of Cosmopolitan Studies.* London: Routledge, 198–207.

Islamoğlu, Huricihan 2012. "Islamicate World Histories" in Douglas Northrup, ed. *A Companion to World History.* Oxford: Blackwell, 447–463.

Islamoğlu, Huricihan 2014 "World History as Fulfillment of Individual Responsibility," Unpublished paper delivered at workshop "Toward an Islamicate cosmopolitan imagination: the moral legacy of Marshall GS Hodgson" at WOCMES, August 18, 2014. METU, Ankara.

Kahn, Joel S. 2008 *Other Malays: Nationalism and Cosmopolitanism in the Modern Malay World.* Honolulu, HI: University of Hawaii Press.

Kamali, Masoud 2006 "Middle Eastern Modernities, Islam, and Cosmopolitanism" in Gerard Delanty,ed. *Europe and Asia beyond East and West.* New York, NY: Routledge, 161–178.

Kamaruzaman, Kamar Oniah 2003 *Early Muslim Scholarship in Religionswissenschaft: The Works and Contributions of Abu-Rayhan Muhammad Ibn Ahmad al-Biruni.* Kuala Lumpur: International Islamic University.

Karim, Karim H. 2011 "Cosmopolitanism: Ways of Being Muslim" in Amyn B. Sajoo, ed. *A Companion to Muslim Cultures.* London: I.B. Tauris, 201–220.

Kersten, Carool 2011 *Cosmopolitans and Heretics: New Muslim Intellectuals and the Study of Islam.* New York, NY: Columbia University Press.

Khazeni, Arash 2014 *Sky Blue Stone: The Turquoise Trade in World History.* Berkeley, CA: University of California Press.

Kozah, Mario 2015 *The Birth of Indology as an Islamic Science. Al-Bīrūnī's Treatise on Yoga Psychology.* Leiden, The Netherlands: Brill.

Kozah, Mario ed. & fr. 2020 *The Yoga Sutras of Patanjali by Abu Rayhan Al- Biruni.* New York, NY: NYU Press.

Kuehn, Thomas 2012 "Translators of Empire: Colonial Cosmopolitanism, Ottoman Bureaucrats, and the Struggle over the Governance of Yemen" in Derryl N. MacLean and Sikeena Karmali Ahmed, eds. *Cosmopolitanisms in Muslim Contexts: Perspectives from the Past*. Edinburgh: Edinburgh University Press, 51–67.

Kreese, Kai. 2012 "Interrogating 'Cosmopolitanism' in an Indian Ocean Setting: Thinking through Mombasa on the Swahili Coast" in Derryl N. MacLean and Sikeena Karmali Ahmed, eds. *Cosmopolitanisms in Muslim Contexts: Perspectives from the Past*. Edinburgh: Edinburgh University Press, 31–50.

LaMotte, Carol, ed. 2008 *Istanbul, Isfahan, Delhi: Three of Islamic Art, Masterpieces from the Louvre Collection*. Istanbul: Sakip Sabanci Muzesi.

Larguèche, Abdelhamid. 2001 "The City and the Sea: Evolving Forms of Mediterranean Cosmopolitanism in Tunis, 1700–1881" in Julia Clancy Smith, ed. *North Africa, Islam, and the Mediterranean World: From the Almoravids to the Algerian War*. New York, NY: Frank Cass Publishers, 117–128.

Lawrence, Bruce B. 2003 "Islamicate Civilization: The View from Asia" in Brannon M. Wheeler, ed. *Teaching Islam*. New York, NY: Oxford University Press, 61–74.

Lawrence, Bruce B. 2005 "Introduction to Ibn Khaldun" in Franz Rosenthal, trans., abridged by N.J. Dawood *The Muqaddimah: An Introduction to History*. Princeton, NJ: Princeton University Press, vii–xxv.

Lawrence, Bruce B. 2006 *The Qur'an: A Biography*. New York, NY: Atlantic Monthly Press.

Lawrence, Bruce B. 2010a "Afterword: Competing Genealogies of Muslim Cosmopolitanism" in Carl W. Ernst and Richard C. Martin, eds. *Rethinking Islamic Studies: From Orientalism to Cosmopolitanism*. Columbia, SC: University of South Carolina Press, 303–323.

Lawrence, Bruce B. 2010b "Islam in Afro-Eurasia: A Bridge Civilization" in Peter J. Katzenstein, ed. *Civilizations in World Politics: Plural and Pluralist Perspectives*. Abingdon, England: Routledge, 157–175.

Lawrence, Bruce B. 2013a "Muslim Engagement with Injustice and Violence" in Mark Juergensmeyer et al., eds. *The Oxford Handbook of Religion and Violence*. New York, NY: Oxford University Press, 126–152.

Lawrence, Bruce B. 2013b "'All Distinctions are Political, Artificial': The Fuzzy Logic of M. F. Husain" *Common Knowledge* 19: 269–274.

Lawrence, Bruce B. 2013c "The Cosmopolitan Canopy of East Maritime SE Asia: Minority Citizenship in the Phil-Indo Archipelago," *Comparative Islamic Studies* 7: 67–104. Reprinted in *East by Mid-East: Studies in Cultural, Historical and Strategic Connectivities*, edited by Anchi Hoh and Brannon Wheeler, 67–104. Sheffield, England: Equinox.

Lawrence, Bruce B. 2014a "Genius Denied and Reclaimed: A 40 Year Retrospect on Marshall G.S. Hodgson's *The Venture of Islam*," available at http://blog.lareviewofbooks.org/larb-channels/genius-denied-reclaimed-40-year-retrospect-marshall-g-s-hodgsons-venture-islam (accessed June 24, 2020).

Lawrence, Bruce B. 2014b "Al-Biruni: Against the Grain," *Critical Muslim* 12: 61–71.

Lawrence, Bruce B. 2015a *Who Is Allah?* Chapel Hill, NC: University of North Carolina Press.

Lawrence, Bruce B. 2015b "Islamicate Cosmopolitan? A Past Without a Future, or a Future Still Unfolding," available at https://humanitiesfutures.org/papers/islamicate-cosmopolitan-past-without-future-future-still-unfolding (accessed June 9, 2020).

Lawrence, Bruce B. 2018 "Islamicate Cosmopolitanism from North Africa to Southeast Asia" in Joshua Gedacht and R. Michael Feener, eds. *Challenging Cosmopolitanism: Coercion, Mobility and Displacement in Islamic Asia*. Edinburgh: Edinburgh University Press, 30–52.

Leichtman, Mara A. and Dorothea Schulz, eds. 2012 "Muslim Cosmopolitanism: Movement, Identity and Contemporary Reconfiguration," Special issue of *City & Society* 24: 1.

Lewis, Reina November 2007 "Consumption and Cosmopolitanism: The Veil, the Body, the Law," first keynote address at the Association of Muslim Social Scientists (AMSS), Third Annual Canadian Regional Conference on "Cosmopolitan Islamic Identity and Thought" at Wilfrid Laurier University (Waterloo, Ontario).

Mabro, Robert 2004 "Alexandria 1860–1960: The Cosmopolitan Identity" in Anthony Hirst and Michael Silk, eds. *Alexandria, Real and Imagined*. Aldershot, England: Ashgate.

Malagaris, George 2019 *Biruni*. Oxford: Oxford University Press.

MacLean, Derryl N. and Sikeena Karmali Ahmed, eds. 2012 *Cosmopolitanisms in Muslim Contexts: Perspectives from the Past*. Edinburgh: Edinburgh University Press.

Maghraoui, Driss 2009 "Reading Secularism in Morocco" in *Langues Et Literatures: Cultural Representations in Morocco*. Rabat: Faculty of Letters and Human Sciences, University Mohammed V, 21–44.

Marlow, Louise 2011 *The Rhetoric of Biography: Narrating Lives in Persianate Societies*. Cambridge, MA: Harvard University Press.

Marsden, Magnus 2008 "Muslim Cosmopolitans? Transnational Life in Northern Pakistan," *Journal of Asian Studies* 67(1): 213–247.

Masud, Muhammad Khalid 2012 "Cosmopolitanism and Authenticity: The Doctrine of *Tashabbuh Bi'l-Kuffar* ("Imitating the Infidel") in Modern South Asian Fatwas" in Derryl N. MacLean and Sikeena Karmali Ahmed, eds. Cosmopolitanisms in Muslim Contexts: Perspectives from the Past. Edinburgh: Edinburgh University Press 156–175.

Melvin-Koushki, Matthew 2018a "Persianate Geomancy from Ṭūsī to the Millennium: A Preliminary Survey" in Nader El-Bizri and Eva Orthmann, eds. *Occult Sciences in Premodern Islamic Culture*. Beirut: Orient-Institut Beirut, 151–199.

Melvin-Koushki, Matthew 2018b "Early Modern Islamicate Empire: New Forms of Religiopolitical Legitimacy" in Armando Salvatore, Roberto Tottoli, and Babak Rahimi, eds. *The Wiley-Blackwell History of Islam*. Chichester, England: Wiley-Blackwell, 353–375.

Melvin-Koushki, Matthew and Noah Gardiner, eds. 2017 "Islamicate Occultism: New Perspectives" special double issue of *Arabica* 64(3–4): 287–693.

Melvin-Koushki, Matthew and James Pickett 2016 "Mobilizing Magic: Occultism in Central Asia and the Continuity of High Persianate Culture under Russian Rule," *Studia Islamica* 111(2): 231–284.

Necipoğlu, Gülru 2012 "The Concept of Islamic Art: Inherited Discourses and New Approaches," *Journal of Art Historiography* 6(June): 1–16.

Oktem, Kerem, "Contours of a New Republic and Signals from the Past: How to Understand Taksim Square," available at http://www.jadaliyya.com/pages/index/12088/contours-of-a-new-republic-and-signals-from-the-past (accessed June 12, 2013).

Osella, Filippo and Caroline Osella 2008 "'I Am Gulf: The Production of Cosmopolitanism in Kozhikode, Kerala, India" in Edward Simpson and Kai Kreese, eds. *Struggling with History: Islam and Cosmopolitanism in the Western Indian Ocean.* New York, NY: Columbia Press, 323–356.

Ostle, Robin 2002 "Alexandria: A Mediterranean Cosmopolitan Center of Cultural Production" in Leila Fawaz, C.A. Bayly, and Robert Ilbert, eds. *Modernity and Culture from the Mediterranean to the Indian Ocean, 1890–1920.* New York, NY: Columbia University Press.

Petrů, Tomáš 2016 "'Lands below the Winds' as Part of the Persian Cosmopolis: An Inquiry into Linguistic and Cultural Borrowings from the Persianate Societies in the Malay World," *Moussons:* 147–161 http://journals.openedition.org/moussons/3572; doi:10.4000/moussons.3572.

Pickett, James 2015 "The Persianate Sphere during the Age of Empires: Islamic Scholars and Networks of Exchange in Central Asia 1747–1917," (PhD dissertation, Princeton University).

Prange, Sebastian, 2016 *Monsoon Islam: Trade and Faith on the Medieval Malabar Coast.* Cambridge: Cambridge University Press.

Ray, Sugata 2019 *Climate Change and the Art of Devotion: Geoaesthetics in the Land of Krishna, 1550–1850.* Seattle, WA: University of Washington Press.

Reese, Scott 2008 "The 'Respectable Citizens' of Shaykh Uthman: Religious Discourse, Trans-locality and the Construction of Local Contexts in Colonial Aden" in Edward Simpson and Kai Kreese, eds. *Struggling with History: Islam and Cosmopolitanism in the Western Indian Ocean.* New York, NY: Columbia Press, 189–222.

Ricci, Ronit 2011 *Islam Translated: Literature, Conversion, and the Arabic Cosmopolis of South and Southeast Asia.* Chicago, IL: University of Chicago Press.

Ridgeon, Lloyd, ed. 2018 *Javanmardi: The Ethics and Practice of Persianate Perfection.* London: Gingko Library.

Roberts, Allen F. and Mary N. Roberts 2004 *A Saint in the City: Sufi Arts of Urban Senegal.* Los Angeles, CA: University of California.

Rozehnal, Robert, ed. 2019 *Piety, Politics, and Everyday Ethics in Southeast Asian Islam: Beautiful Behavior.* London and New York, NY: Bloomsbury Academic.

Bibliography

Salvatore, Armando 2016 *The Sociology of Islam: Knowledge, Power and Civility*. Chichester, England: Wiley-Blackwell.

Salvatore, Armando, with Roberto Tottoli and Babak Rahimi, eds. 2018 *The Wiley-Blackwell History of Islam*. Chichester, England: Wiley-Blackwell.

Salzman, Ariel 2012 "Islampolis, Cosmopolis: Ottoman Urbanity between Myth, Memory, and Postmodernity" in Derryl N. MacLean and Sikeena Karmali Ahmed, eds. *Cosmopolitanisms in Muslim Contexts: Perspectives from the Past*. Edinburgh: Edinburgh University Press, 68–91.

Shaw, Wendy M.K. 2019 *What Is "Islamic" Art? Between Religion and Perception*. Cambridge: Cambridge University Press.

Simpson, Edward and Kai Kreese 2008 "Introduction: Cosmopolitanism Contested: Anthropology and History in the Western Indian Ocean" in Edward Simpson and Kai Keese, eds. *Struggling with History: Islam and Cosmopolitanism in the Western Indian Ocean*. New York, NY: Columbia Press, 1–37.

Spooner, Brian and William L. Hanaway 2012 *Literacy in the Persianate World-Writing and the Social Order*. Philadelphia, PA: University of Pennsylvania Museum of Archeology and Anthropology.

Starr, Deborah 2008 *Remembering Cosmopolitan Egypt: Culture, Society and Empire*. Abingdon, England: Routledge.

Starr, Deborah 2005 "Recuperating Cosmopolitan Alexandria: Circulation of Narratives and Narratives of Circulation," *Cities* 22(3): 217–228.

Stoker, Gerry, Andrew Mason, Anthony McGrew, Chris Armstrong, David Owen, Graham Smith, Momoh Banya, Derek McGee, and Clare Saunders 2012 *Prospects for Citizenship*. Qatar: Bloomsbury Academic.

Tamari, Salim, 2011 "Confessionalism and Public Space in Ottoman and Colonial Jerusalem" in Diane E. Davis and Nora Libertun de Duren, eds. *Cities and Sovereignty. Identity Politics in Urban Spaces*. Bloomington and Indianapolis, IN: Indiana University Press, 59–82.

Tuominen, Pekka 2013 "The Clash of Values across Symbolic Boundaries: Claims of Urban Space in Contemporary Istanbul," *Contemporary Islam: Dynamics of Muslim Life* 7: 33–51.

Bibliography

Van der Veer, Peter 2002 "Colonial Cosmopolitanism" in Steven Vertovec and Robin Cohen, eds. *Conceiving Cosmopolitanism: Theory, Context, and Practice*. New York, NY: Oxford University Press, 165–179.

Van der Veer, Peter 2004 "Cosmopolitan Option" in Jonathan Friedman and Shalini Randeria, eds. *Worlds on the Move: Globalization, Migration, and Cultural Security*, London: I.B. Tauris, 167–178.

Wagoner, Phillip B. 1996 "'Sultan among Hindu Kings': Dress, Titles, and the Islamicization of Hindu Culture at Vijayanagara," *Journal of Asian Studies* 55(4): 851–880.

Wagoner, Phillip B. 2000 "Harihara, Bukka, and the Sultan: The Delhi Sultanate in the Political Imagination of Vijayanagara" in David Gilmartin and Bruce B. Lawrence, eds. *Beyond Turk and Hindu: Rethinking Religious Identities in Islamicate South Asia*. Gainesville, FL: University Press of Florida, 300–326.

Wescoat, James, Jr. 2019 "'In the Centre of the Map...': Reflecting on Marshall Hodgson's Ideas about Conscience and History in the Architectural Experience of Humayun," *South Asian Studies* 35(1): 7–24.

Zaman, Qasim Muhammad 2005 "The Scope and Limits of Islamic Cosmopolitanism and the Discursive Language of the *'Ulama*" in miriam cooke and Bruce B. Lawrence, eds. *Muslim Networks from Hajj to Hip Hop*. Chapel Hill, NC: University of North Carolina Press, 84–104.

Zubaida, Sami 1999 "Cosmopolitanism and the Middle East" in Roel Meijer, ed. *Cosmopolitanism, Identity, and Authenticity in the Middle East*. Richmond, England: Curzon Press,15–34.

Zubaida, Sami 2002 "Middle Eastern Experiences of Cosmopolitanism" in Steven Vertovec and Robin Cohen, eds. *Conceiving Cosmopolitanism: Theory, Context, and Practice*. New York, NY: Oxford University Press, 32–41.

Index

Note: Page numbers followed by "*f*" refers to figures and page numbers followed by "n" refers to endnotes.

Islamicate Cosmopolitan Spirit, First Edition. Bruce B. Lawrence.
© 2021 Bruce B. Lawrence. Published 2021 by John Wiley & Sons, Ltd.

143